Unexpected

Cover Design: Greg Jackson, Thinkpen Deisgn

Published by Barbour Books, an imprint of Barbour Publishing, Inc., 1810 Barbour Drive, Uhrichsville, Ohio 44683, www.barbourbooks.com

Our mission is to inspire the world with the life-changing message of the Bible.

Member of the
Evangelical Christian
Publishers Association

Printed in China.

Valorie Quesenberry

Unexpected

Devotions & Prayers
for a Delighted Soul

BARBOUR BOOKS
An Imprint of Barbour Publishing, Inc.

Introduction

I don't like to be surprised. I'm not exactly what one might call a control freak, but I do appreciate planning. This characteristic no doubt prohibits me from experiencing some of the joy in life that comes from spontaneity. I'm sure I have missed opportunities to relax and enjoy because of my angst at not knowing what was going to happen.

Perhaps you can identify with that. Maybe you also like to plan ahead and be prepared for what's coming. Or maybe you have the rare ability to adapt at a moment's notice. Maybe for you the sudden shift in plans or the reroute of your schedule is less about what you can't do and more about a new opportunity.

Whichever category you fit in, go on this journey of discovery with me as we look at the unexpected moments in our lives and discover what God is up to in them. We'll look at some surprise moments in the Bible and see how ancient people of faith responded. We'll discuss the promises of God that will hold us steady in our own unexpected moments. And we'll remember that some of those moments are actually positive, and we'll embrace the delight that comes from them.

Come along with me. Prepare to be surprised!

UNEXPECTED MERCY

Put Out the Fire

*For lack of wood the fire goes out, and where
there is no whisperer, contention ceases.*
PROVERBS 26:20 AMPC

I've always been a wordy person. Some of that is just how God made
me. Some of it is that my parents shaped me to love books and words.
As a writer, words are my tools, my product, my ministry. And words
sometimes get me in trouble.

Because I use words professionally, I have honed the ability to
make them convey the emotion I want in particular settings. They are
powerful things, filled with the ability to bring hope or despair, praise
or condemnation, love or anger, peace or frustration. But occasionally I
misuse them or convey a message I didn't realize was coming through.

Those who observe what's happened respond to me in various
ways, depending on their relationship to me. Some admonish. Some
rebuke. Some sympathize. Some smirk. Some rejoice. Some smolder.
Some retaliate.

But some give grace.

Perhaps there is no more loving gift for a writer than that of grace.
My husband has done this for me on more than one occasion when
my poorly communicated message created a firestorm. He has picked
up the pieces of me, soothed my horror, and assured me that I would
write again (though I vowed I never would). This is grace.

And it is something we can give to others on a regular basis.

Who among us has not misspoken? Who has not meant the right thing and said it wrongly? Who has not embarrassed herself with her words? Who has not realized how something sounded until after it left her lips? Many would rather pin you to the wall than help you hide your embarrassment. Many would use your discomfort to their advantage.

But what if we model another way?

What does it hurt to "not hear"? Why can't we refuse to latch onto those hurtful things? Why can't we, as my mother used to say, "let it go in one ear and out the other"?

Let's try giving unexpected mercy.

Let the words fade away. Don't try to hang on to them, remember them, or enshrine them.

I once heard a friend say, "Hurtful words are like mud. If you try to rub it off when it's fresh, it smears and sets in. But if you leave it alone and let it dry, you can flick it off with a fingernail."

Show unexpected mercy. Douse the flame. Put out the fire.

Father God, help me today to show mercy by "not noticing" the misspeaks and blunders of others. I want to ease their discomfort and not make it worse by my reaction. Thank You for understanding every word I speak and knowing my unseen motives. In Jesus' name, amen.

Grace Day

For by grace you have been saved through faith, and that not of yourselves.
EPHESIANS 2:8 NKJV

I'm a confirmed bibliophile. That's not something bad. In basic English, it means "bookworm." I've loved the library since my father first took me to the Argie Cooper Public Library in Shelbyville, Tennessee, and helped me get my first library card. It was one of those old ornate, brick buildings, the Carnegie-type library, with a cupola and huge cement steps, and it smelled of weathered paper and centuries-old bindings. I can still remember that aroma—the scent of adventure hidden in thousands of unread pages. Week after week I happily selected books about girl sleuth Nancy Drew, pixie-haired detective Trixie Belden, spunky nurse Cherry Ames, and those intrepid siblings, the Bobbsey twins. And then I discovered other writers and other series and found more journeys waiting for me on every shelf. My love affair with reading is still going strong.

As a young mom, I determined that my kids would learn to love the library. I started taking my firstborn when she was a preschooler and kept visiting as more babies came. Thursday was library day in our home, and we'd get our library bags (they were special, just for books), load up the minivan, and go searching for treasure. When they started school, we'd stop at the library on the way home. I required "learning books" (five on every library trip) as well as storybooks, and it amazed me to see the topics in which they were interested—sharks and insects and space exploration and history. Those are mother-children times I still cherish. And maybe my children will institute a library day with their own children someday.

A definite downside to taking several children to the library and also checking out books yourself is keeping up with the due dates. When we all went on the same day every week, it was manageable. But if we ever got out of rhythm, it could be expensive. Let's just say that our family has made sizable contributions to the continuation of public libraries in several states. May their mission live on! I learned to smile and pay.

Imagine my delight when one day I discovered that the local library had a "grace day"—an extra day before fines kicked in! To tell you the truth, I still felt guilty for not being on time, but who is going to reject grace? Actually, a lot of people do. But grace is what the cross is all about.

You're guilty, caught, because you didn't live up to the rules. But God surprises you with grace—mercy because Jesus paid the penalty. Every day in God's kingdom is grace day. I can't think of anything better than accepting that offer.

God, thank You for unexpected mercy. Thank You for
the cross. Thank You for this grace day. Amen.

When He Cushions the Crunch

*The Lord is merciful and gracious, slow to anger
and plenteous in mercy and loving-kindness.*
Psalm 103:8 AMPC

Nothing is as stomach sickening as hearing the crunch of metal and fiberglass when the vehicle you're driving collides with an object or another vehicle. Unfortunately, I have heard this sound on more than one occasion. Some of them stay strongly in my memory.

I was a young mom on my way to pick up my eldest at elementary school with my preschooler in her car seat. I leaned down to pick up something, swerved inadvertently into the lane beside me on the interstate, and sideswiped another vehicle.

Another occasion wasn't quite as dangerous. It was the first Sunday in our new home. My husband, the pastor, was already at the church ready to greet the parishioners and fill his new role. I finished Sunday dinner prep, got myself ready, finished helping my four children, packed them into the minivan, and started to back out of the garage. But I remembered that we didn't have a remote garage door opener yet, and so I needed to go in the side door, close the garage, and then get back in the van and drive to church. Somehow, in my harried, befuddled mind, I thought I could leave the driver's side door open and back out! Go figure. The horrifying bending and twisting of the door let me know I was wrong! I didn't make it to church that Sunday morning! I couldn't even get my door closed.

Another time I was on my way to pick up my children at school and stopped to get gasoline on the way. Hurrying through the process, I jumped back in the van and took off and scraped against the concrete island of the gas station!

On another occasion I was on the interstate in rush-hour traffic, distracted by an embarrassing situation that had occurred a short while before. All lanes were stop and go, and as I slowed down, I glanced at my phone and smacked slowly into the truck in front of me. My vehicle received only a slight crack from that one, and the other driver's vehicle was fine.

Then, on a wintry December evening, my daughter and I were on the way to a funeral home in a rural area. Once again, my husband, the pastor, was already there. The roads were covered with snow, hazardous. Trying to share the road with an approaching vehicle, I skittered onto the shoulder and started sliding. There was no stopping it. We spun around in the road and landed with a *kerthump* in a field on the opposite side. A couple of hours and friendly neighbors with trucks later, we were out and on the way home—with no damage to my minivan!

That's mercy—when you expect the worst and it doesn't happen. Or when you understand later how bad it could have been and wasn't.

God shows up in unexpected ways in our lives often enough that we know He can do anything. Other times we feel the effect of the way He created our world—the laws of physics are in force, and they hold true. And the fallenness of creation ensures that negative results are, many times, the norm. But sometimes He steps in and reroutes the path of the storm or cushions the impact of the crash or smooths away the contours of the tumor, and we remember, once again, that all things bow to His will. That's our unexpectedly merciful Father.

～◦◦～

*Heavenly Father, I praise You for the ways You show up
in unexpected mercy in my life. Most of all, I thank You for
the mercy I've received through Jesus. Amen.*

Mercy for Guilt

*And Jesus said unto her, Neither do
I condemn thee: go, and sin no more.*
JOHN 8:11 KJV

A death sentence commuted. You can't get more mercy than that.

Perhaps no biblical story has been cited more often as an example of the mercy and grace of Jesus than the account of the woman caught in adultery, a violation of God's law, clearly sin. Jesus never disputes that fact. He knew she had sinned. And He knew she did it intentionally, for He later told her not to do it again. He knows hearts.

What sins have you committed that Jesus knows about? Does today find you guilty? Maybe, just like her, you have been found out. Maybe today your shame is being made public, to your family, husband, friends, church. Maybe every hiding place is gone, and you feel, like her, thrown down in the sand before the eyes of people who haven't done what you have. Maybe you're shivering like her, with only a blanket thrown around you to hide the naked state in which you were found (or at least it feels that way emotionally).

I have wondered what she felt. What was it like to see the holy, loving eyes of Jesus turn to her? She probably hung her head, averted her eyes. She was guilty and deserved death. And she knew it.

Jesus spoke, not to her, but to the men. "If you haven't ever sinned, throw a stone." Then He stooped and wrote with His finger in the sand. And because they couldn't get Him to do what they wanted, the bad guys drifted off, leaving the problem with Jesus. Let Him deal with it.

Jesus rose and looked again at her and asked if anyone still accused her. But no one there was without sin—except Him. He was sinless, but He didn't throw a stone; He did something unexpected. Instead of handing down a death sentence, He offered mercy and restoration. And a command: "Go and sin no more."

What happened then? Did Jesus walk with her back to her home so she wouldn't be a woman alone in a culture where she was suspect? Did He talk to her on the way and encourage her to live a new life?

Maybe. For a man to speak publicly with a woman was socially unacceptable at that time, but Jesus cared more for people than practice. He was the source of everything unexpectedly merciful. And He is still.

Lord God, thank You for the divine mercy You showed in Jesus. Today I ask for forgiveness and accept Your offer of freedom from sin. In Christ's name, amen.

The Emergency Brake

Whoever is slow to anger is better than the mighty,
and he who rules his spirit than he who takes a city.
PROVERBS 16:32 ESV

My grandfather used to say, "Patience is the ability to idle your motor when you feel like stripping your gears."

Ah yes, patience. That elusive phantom control we long for. We blame many things for its absence—environment, genetics, mood, hormones, family, weather, and more. And there are many contributing factors, to be sure.

But when it comes down to the nitty-gritty of life, patience is an action, not a feeling, and it is only truly possible with the enabling power of the Holy Spirit at work in our personalities. He empowers us to respond appropriately even if we feel differently. We often do not choose to let Him help us. We find it more satisfactory to react to the insult or irritation or provocation. But we display holy growth when we submit in the moment and respond not out of self-centeredness but out of mature, godly love.

In this way, we can show unexpected mercy to those whom God has placed in our lives. Those around us have been conditioned to expect retaliation from others, withdrawal, the "cold shoulder," the "silent treatment." What if, instead of following the appetites of the carnal mind, which Romans 8:7 says is against God, we purposefully daily follow the will of the Spirit? What if we affirmed our big moment of total surrender with a lifetime of daily surrender?

An emergency brake is a mechanical brake system that completely bypasses the hydraulics of the regular vehicular brakes. In the event of a failure in the normal braking system, the emergency brake can help you get your vehicle safely stopped.

All of us have moments when our normal, calming techniques fail. In that extremity, we need a power that bypasses our human limitations. The writer of Proverbs knew about this, for he wrote that one who can rule over her own spirit is a mightier warrior than the conqueror of a city.

Let's take up the challenge today. Let's embody the unexpected mercy that God gives through us. Let's smile at the slow cashier, not honk or glare at the irritating driver, be kind to the forgetful waitress, swallow the sarcastic retort to our spouse, hug our moody teenager, love our world through patience. The old adage is true: "People need loving the most when they deserve it the least."

Be the "unexpected" in someone's life today.

Father God, You have been the most unexpected blessing in my life. You loved me before I knew You, gave grace to me when I was a rebel, and have had more patience with me than I could ever merit. I ask You, through the power of Your Holy Spirit, to enable me to choose Your way in my moments of irritation today. I want my life to be a daily walk of surrender and beautiful response to Your way. In Jesus' name, amen.

He Sees Dark Places

The eyes of the L<small>ORD</small> are in every place.
P<small>ROVERBS</small> 15:3 <small>KJV</small>

I didn't expect the phone call. We had been having a fun Friday evening with friends. Though it was the fateful week of September 11, 2001, we were managing to squeeze joy out of togetherness with another pastor and his wife and their little girl. I was the mom of a six-year-old, almost-four-year-old, and sixteen-month-old. My husband was busy in ministry. We were stunned with the national news, patriotism blooming in our hearts, the rush of compassion for our fellow citizens strong. But things were about to get much more personal.

My youngest brother, twenty-three years old, had been in a terrible crash on his motorcycle and was being flown to a trauma unit in a distant city. His condition was critical.

Such news is ingested in a rush, and then the brain backs up and refuses to move quickly. You're stuck somewhere between "This can't be real" and "What do I need to do now?" The thought that came and lodged in my mind was the image of my little brother lying somewhere on a road, bleeding and alone. My husband held me while I tried to process the situation. We decided to make a middle-of-the-night trip to be with my family at the hospital. We packed, we drove, we arrived for one of the most difficult seasons for all of us.

The other side of the story, years later, is that God spared my brother's life, miraculously soothed the effects of a traumatic brain injury, restored his ability to speak and walk and function in life. And today he holds a job, teaches Sunday school, plays piano at church, and reminds us by his presence that there is nothing too hard for the

Lord. Does my brother still deal with challenges from the incident? Sure. But miracles happened; God showed mercy.

Sometimes the crash is fatal, the swelling doesn't stop, the restoration doesn't happen, the earthly miracle doesn't appear. Sometimes unexpected events bring an unexpected type of mercy—the kind we don't want but God nonetheless gives.

Perhaps one of the most beautiful things I learned in the aftermath is that God always sees the unexpected things. When my brother rammed into a utility pole on a rural road, God was there. When hijackers commandeered planes and hurtled them into tall buildings, God was there. There is no dark place where His eyes cannot see. And what is unexpected to us is His laboratory, His best place to show up.

There is no way to avoid unexpected crisis phone calls and events. But there is a way to prepare for them. Stay in communion with the heavenly Father and expect His eyes to be watching.

Lord, thank You for being ever present and ever watchful and ever merciful. Nothing unexpected can change those realities. Amen.

Don't Fight over Pebbles

*"By this all will know that you are My disciples,
if you have love for one another."*
JOHN 13:35 NKJV

I once was in a daily situation with someone who was on the hunt to catch me making mistakes. Ever been there? This individual was critical of my Christian walk and took delight in anything that might prove I was doing something wrong. I don't have to tell you that this is never the attitude of someone who follows Christ. You and I are called to a different level of interaction with those around us.

Jesus lived for thirty-three years on this earth with fallen people, people who made mistakes every day. How do you think He responded to that? We know that He was the perfect Son of God. I don't know if that means He never made an error in learning as a child. I do know it means He never transgressed the laws of God; He never sinned.

Sin and mistakes are like boulders and pebbles. Often when we hear the Christian community speak about showing grace to those around us, we hear them lump together willful sin and human error. True, both are short of perfection. But it is also true that motive is significant. If my toddler knocks over her glass of milk while eating, my response is different than if she looks me in the eye and pours out her milk in defiance. The result is the same—spilled milk, a mess—but motive makes a big difference.

Motive makes a big difference in our relationship with God too and in our relationship with others. Our response to those who grieve us should be grace no matter their motives, but the pebbles probably don't even merit our attention.

Our world is very unforgiving. I've heard people complain and gripe about small insults that they should just step over. "If she wants me to be nice to her, she'd better apologize—I'll tell you that!" Really? If a big boulder is blocking communication in the relationship, then address it and try to get it removed. But can you really not ignore the pebbles littering the path?

Relationships are hard enough; don't clutch those little pebbles for dear life. The other person might not even realize what happened. And probably their motive was never to hurt you.

What makes a Christ follower different is the love she shows. That's what Jesus said. Can you show unexpected mercy today in a way that will point others to Him? Ignoring the pebbles will make you stand out in any crowd you're in.

God, I know that humanly I tend to be self-protective. I ask You to give me the power today to ignore the pebbles in my relationships so that Your light can shine unexpectedly through me. In Jesus' name, amen.

UNEXPECTED GROWTH

A Better Way

"Your heavenly Father knows that you need them all."
MATTHEW 6:32 ESV

A self-employed friend of mine says that whenever he and his wife experienced a financial need, God usually didn't send a check but another opportunity for work. Can you relate?

I recall a time when our family was in actual financial distress. We were in a ministry situation with limited resources, and my husband's search for additional employment had turned up nothing—for months. God supplied food to eat; we didn't starve. We had a place to live and the basics, but very basic. There were some things I thought we needed that we couldn't get. And God didn't get us out of that for a little while.

I learned a lot during that season. One of the most significant lessons was that God supplies our needs according to His description, not ours. What we think we need is not necessarily what we do need to fulfill His will at that particular time. Another lesson I can see in retrospect is that when our bank account was not miraculously blooming, we were growing in other ways.

I begged God to work things out the way it seemed best to me. But He didn't. He didn't give me the quarter for the gumball machine. Instead, He let me wait until He worked things out in a better way.

You will always have some area of personal growth where the Father is digging around the roots of your soul and exposing what needs to be tended. We expect Him to work above the surface, but He often chooses the deep layers. So don't think that He isn't concerned with the things you can see. In my experience, instead of giving us the easy, obvious solution—cash flow—He worked on our faith and discipline. He will do the same for you. If you are His child, you are never out of His awareness. He is interested in you at the soul level. And He is always perfecting something in you.

Lord, thank You for being deeply involved in my personal growth. You have promised to give me what I need to glorify You today. I love You and trust You. Amen.

Not Straight Lines

You number my wanderings.
PSALM 56:8 NKJV

I like to drive on country roads. They meander and curve and laze around hills and dip by wooded hollows and climb onto ridges. Driving in the country is a pleasure, an adventure, a sensory treat. And though interstate highway driving is straight and fast, it brings little joy.

The shortest distance between two points, they say, is a straight line, which is mathematically proven to be true. But often God refuses to put us on the straight path and chooses for us the curvy one instead.

When we zoom from one life experience, one season, one victory straight to another, we can become arrogant, content, and comfortable. So God shakes up the map, and we discover the delight of bends in the road and forced deceleration in speed.

The word *wandering* generally carries a negative tone. People of purpose do not wander. The Bible does not speak well of those who wander. The Israelites wandered in the desert for forty years as discipline for their rebellion and lack of faith. The wisdom literature of the Bible tells us that wandering is not a desirable state of being, either emotionally or spiritually. Yet at times, God lets us wander. And it is for our good.

From wandering we learn that it's okay not to know the entire route we're walking. From wandering we learn that some lessons are best understood when we seem to go in circles. From wandering we learn that God is Lord of every journey and that He decides how quickly to get us to our destination.

One of the delights of driving on a country road are the landmarks—old school buildings, white wood-sided churches, faded barns, glorious farmhouses, vintage roadside parks, and historical sites. They're more than eye candy. They're stories in visual form. Behind every one of them is a tale of life, love, and learning, of hardship, sacrifice, and joy. Someone cared enough to carve out a place to live, a place to share with others, a place with meaning.

And these unexpected vignettes are what God uses in our spiritual journey too. When you feel like you can't find the "yellow brick road" to Oz, God may be letting you wander a bit so He can teach you wonderful, unexpected things along the way.

Stay on the journey. The sidetrack you're taking right now has a purpose.

Heavenly Father, I know I can trust Your leadership. If I follow Your voice, You will get me to the place I need to be and teach me new things along the way. Amen.

Let the Flowers Bloom

*"For behold, the winter is past; the rain is over and gone.
The flowers appear on the earth, the time of singing has come."*
SONG OF SOLOMON 2:11–12 ESV

Wildflowers spring up in amazing places. As I drive along the interstate, I am amazed at the beauty of random (to my eye) fields of wildflowers. Perhaps somebody sows the seeds at some time in an effort to keep our highways beautiful. But in some places they simply come up from some hidden richness below, bringing color and cheer to our world.

We must encourage flowers to grow in our hearts. Weeds of sin try to choke them out, and pollutants in our souls work to kill them at the roots. We must cultivate the soil of our lives to be fertile and receptive.

I remember a time in our family's life when we had been hurt by a ministry situation. The circumstances for our family's future were greatly changed, and all of us were devastated. Even our children were going through the sad process of giving away pets and saying goodbye to best friends as we prepared to move. My husband and I did our best to get through those difficult transitional months. We tried to process the disappointment properly and biblically. We knew that we had to allow the flowers to bloom again, so to speak. We were not going to be able to go back; we had to look ahead, to let happy feelings take root as we put positive patterns in place for our future health. We had cried long enough. The rainy days needed to be over and gone. It was time for flowers and singing.

We can choose to make our future brighter as we base our decisions not on our feelings but on the realization that God has called us to make choices that encourage growth in our spiritual lives. We can deliberately choose to put our hope in God even when we aren't feeling hopeful. We can purposefully clear away the weeds and let the flowers poke through.

I don't know what has happened in the field of your life, what unexpected calamity has brought a season of rain. But I do know that God calls us to open our eyes to the season of flowers. Let it come when it's time. Don't stay in the rain. Listen: the birds are starting to sing.

Dear Father, I'm glad You understand the seasons in our lives. Thank You for bringing me through a difficult time. Now I turn to the time for flowers and ask You to help me cultivate joy again in my life. In Jesus' name, amen.

Peace, Not Power

*So then let us pursue what makes
for peace and for mutual upbuilding.*
ROMANS 14:19 ESV

Even fairy-tale marriages have conflict. Remember that legendary couple, Jack Sprat who could eat no fat and his wife who could eat no lean?

Of course, no background information is given, so we're not sure why they chose their respective diets. But with all the controversy over fad diets, it's not hard to imagine! For whatever reason, Jack and his wife had opposite menus.

Remember the rest of that nursery rhyme? "And so, betwixt them both, they licked the platter clean." They worked together, they found a solution, and both were satisfied.

Why can't we do the same?

As married people, our differences are supposed to work for us, not against us. It's amazing how God puts attraction in us for someone who we don't even realize is so radically opposite until after the wedding. Before the ceremony, we capitalize on our similarities. "Isn't it awesome that we both like. . . ?" We tend to downplay any differences we start to detect. We can do that during our dating days because we don't have to see them all the time. But after the honeymoon, we can't ignore the differences because they affect how we do life together—everything from the toilet lid to the thermostat to the need for words or silence or hugs.

But God means for our differences to make us work together, to figure out a solution, to paint a complete picture. He puts this opportunity for unexpected growth into every marriage. If we let our oppositeness pull us apart, we're not doing things God's way; we're focusing on self, not on being a couple.

An online article I read urged readers to reach for peace and not power in a marriage. That resonated with me. How often do I sabotage my own relationship with my husband because I'm valuing power (my own way or my own comfort or convenience) over peace?

If you and I were the architects of marriage, we'd have designed it differently. But we're not; God is. And He knows that one of the delightful surprises in that relationship is that life springs from death, unity follows self-denial, and differences can pull us together. I dare you to try it today!

Father, You designed marriage and my husband and me. Today I want to pursue what makes for peace and find the surprising joy in our oppositeness. I ask for Your grace to follow through. In Jesus' name, amen.

Sitting on Eggs

My frame was not hidden from you, when I was being made
in secret, intricately woven in the depths of the earth.
PSALM 139:15 ESV

Wondering how on earth to connect with your child? Why does she think this way? Why can't he understand this? Concerned because of learning problems or personality quirks or surprising traits?

You're not alone.

Thomas Edison's mother, Nancy, probably had the same fears. The great genius was a poor student as a child and engaged in odd behavior, such as sitting on a neighbor's duck eggs to see if he could hatch them. Because his school experience was so bad, she took him out of formal education and taught him at home. How could his elementary school teachers have guessed that someday every classroom in the country would be lit by lightbulbs that traced back to Edison's discoveries and research?

Children are surprise packages. You never know quite what you're getting. Some would tell us today that we should take control over that—everything from genetic abnormalities to the gender and eye color we'd like them to have. But God, the Creator, says He knows best what to give us. And how we are astounded time after time as they grow and more of their personhood and gifting is revealed!

Mothering is a task that requires a stalwart spirit. Mothers are not allowed to be surprised even though we daily are. Mothers must hold it together when a new allergy develops or a new behavior appears, when a sudden change in schedule happens or an unexplained meltdown occurs. Mothers must walk into conversations from which angels would shrink and try to find answers to problems that would astound the great minds of history. And we have a Father in heaven who will help us with every bit of it.

A great woman I looked up to said that she always prayed when something unexpected came up in raising her children. "Lord, You know about Johnny. What should I do about this, Lord?" God always helped her find an answer—whether dealing with a prodigal or learning to do home speech therapy.

I love this reminder that I can trust the One who gave me my children to help me know how best to raise them, discipline them, love them, and guide them. In the unexpected scenarios of parenting, God gives growth—to our children and to us.

Lord God, I can't mother my children without Your help.
Give me grace and wisdom for the unexpected
things, and help me to grow. Amen.

Change My Season

To every thing there is a season,
and a time to every purpose under the heaven.
ECCLESIASTES 3:1 KJV

In every season, I reach a point where I'm ready for the next one. And it's generally way before the weather starts to change accordingly. On frigid winter mornings, I anticipate green shoots in the flower bed. When blustery April breezes make me chilled, I long for warm summer dusks. Working in the garden on a hot day, I think about fall leaves and pumpkins. What is coming seems to eclipse what is happening now.

Yet I get less anxious for seasonal change as I get older. Life itself teaches us that there is beauty in every week of the year—varying kinds of beauty, but beauty all the same. And as we watch our bodies change and our children grow up and leave, we learn to cherish every single mundane moment.

In the Creator's wisdom, He chose to have earthly life continue through a cycle of growth. Seeds are planted then grow. Babies are born then grow, mature, and give birth to other babies. The forests and oceans and plains rejuvenate and recycle. All of nature has a pattern on which it continues.

In our seasons as women, we grow as well. It is easy to look behind or ahead and wish for something else. When we're young, we want to reach that age of mature womanhood and independence, to be married to a loving man and have the joy of children. As we reach middle age, we start to look backward and long for days of youthfulness and purposefulness. But there is something to be learned here, now. There is unexpected growth for today.

I often tell my children, "All God's seasons are good." This goes for biological seasons as well as relational and family and ministry/career seasons. In every one of them, we are captivated by grace and shocked by God's care.

Today probably finds you wishing to change something in your life as a woman or mom—a college degree or romantic relationship, baby weight or wrinkles, or potty training or teen woes—but God asks you to lean back into His surprising growth in today. Today's season is good.

Father, You do all things well. Thank You for the season I'm in today. Help me to use it well and to glorify You in it. In Jesus' name, amen.

Discover Your Tools

Tell Priscilla and Aquila hello. They have been my fellow workers in the affairs of Christ Jesus.

Romans 16:3 TLB

Priscilla was a New Testament woman helping her husband in ministry. Being in a teaching position was unusual for a woman in that culture, yet the New Testament makes reference to her ministry several times. She and her husband, Aquila, mentored the teacher Apollos and were coworkers with the apostle Paul.

What door of ministry has God recently opened for you? Did it surprise you?

As Christian women, we hear a lot about following God's plan for our lives. We try to figure out what He wants us to do; we pray and read books and work on discovering our gifts and talents. Sometimes God's call is obvious, sometimes not.

I wonder what it was like for Priscilla. Was teaching something she'd always loved? Or did it just happen one day and she found out she enjoyed it? Did she feel limited by the biases of her culture?

Whatever Priscilla's experience was, she probably never dreamed she'd be spoken of in the Bible that generations of people would read. She couldn't have imagined that her little part in Paul's life's work would be recorded and read about by women in cultures thousands of years later.

When we answer God's call, He goes beyond what we expect. He takes what we offer and expands and multiplies it just as Jesus did with a little boy's lunch one day.

What do you have to give today to do God's will? A computer

screen? Diaper bag? Homework? Teacher's desk? Stethoscope? File drawer? Canning jars? Home business?

Use the tool God has given you for today. Has He put before you an opportunity to serve in a new way? Pray and try. You may grow in ways you'd never believe. And the record of what you do may inspire someone else.

Lord, take the ways I know I can serve and the unexpected ways You're going to show me, and let me use them for Your glory. Grow me today as I follow You. Amen.

UNEXPECTED TEARS

Rare Beauty

Even to your old age I am He, and even to
hair white with age will I carry you.
Isaiah 46:4 AMPC

They say that the eldest daughter usually assumes the care of aging parents. That would be me. I'm the only daughter of my parents. When this season fully comes, I know I will be there for them. As will my brothers.

Perhaps one of the unexpected challenges of your own aging process is seeing your father and mother decline in health and vigor, physical and mental. As a teen and young adult, your parents seemed indestructible, stable, a part of life you don't question. Sometimes a medical diagnosis changes that and one of them is taken early. But if not, you recognize one day that the natural processes are at work and your mom and dad are getting grayer, smaller, and weaker. It's not a welcome moment.

Aging is natural, at least in our fallen world. I like to remember that if not for the curse of sin that has ruined the way things are supposed to be, we would never have to contend with wrinkles and baldness and sagging jowls. But the second law of thermodynamics is in force, and all things tend toward degeneration.

Joshua, Israel's second great commander, acknowledged this when he gathered the tribal leaders and officials around him and told them that he was "going the way of all the earth" (Joshua 23:14 AMPC). Aging and death are the natural processes of our earth until

Christ comes and all things are changed.

I don't like aging myself, and I certainly don't like to see it happen in those I love. But I am reminded that there is stark beauty even in that. In the book of Isaiah, we are promised that the Lord will carry us even into our old age. The golden hue of our Christ-committed souls can be revealed only in the latter years of life. As my parents one day become blue veined and stooped, their spirits will soar in new ways. Who says that old age cannot be beautiful? Seen from eternity, the senior years are only a passageway.

I love the words of this verse in an old hymn whose authorship is noted only by "K" in the original.

> *Even down to old age all My people shall prove*
> *My sovereign, eternal, unchangeable love;*
> *And when hoary hairs shall their temples adorn,*
> *Like lambs they shall still in My bosom be borne.*

Heavenly Father, thank You for caring for us through every stage of life. I trust You for myself and for those I love that as we go the way of all the earth, we will find unexpected glory and beauty in Your constant presence. In Jesus' name, amen.

Grieving the Pieces

What therefore God hath joined together,
let not man put asunder.
MARK 10:9 KJV

If marriage is a fifty-fifty arrangement, then dividing it up at some point when things get bad might seem logical. But marriage, created by God, is designed as a 100 percent couple thing—they are no more two, but one, said Jesus in Matthew 19:6. Divorce rips apart one being, one whole. That's why it hurts so much. Even those who are forced into divorce by various circumstances and decisions beyond their control will feel that ripping. God made marriage to last for a lifetime, and He meant it to bind a man and woman so deeply that they actually become part of each other.

But divorce happens. Unwanted. Unplanned. Unexpected.

The wording used here by the old King James English—"asunder"—images to me what divorce is. It literally means "in pieces." The Old English carried the idea of being "in a separate place." That's what divorce does—it breaks a home into pieces and puts the "one flesh" in separate places. I know that sometimes after you've had an intense disagreement, that sounds lovely. But it's not. Each of you might need some alone time, but you don't need to be in separate places permanently.

But what do you do when it happens anyway, and you can't change it?

The God who wrote in Malachi 2:16 that He hates divorce also says in Psalm 147:3 that He heals the brokenhearted and binds up their wounds. The Father God we know from scripture reaches out for us. He hears our sobs. He notices our broken hearts. He moves in to be close to us if we let Him.

There is no easy fix. Anyone who has tried to recover from divorce will tell you that. But there is a road to redemption—redemption of heart, of emotions, of hope, of a future.

"Is there anything too hard for Me?" God asked in Jeremiah 32:27 (NKJV).

Of course not.

I don't know how He will bind up your wounds. It will probably look different than the story of someone you know. But He will do it, a little at a time, if you bring those pieces to Him. It's a process, a journey. And you can begin today.

Father God, I ask You to begin Your redeeming work in me today. My heart has been fragmented by divorce—either in my home or in the home of someone close to me. I grieve the ripping apart that has happened. Please heal the brokenhearted and show the path to wholeness, one step at a time. Show me the areas of my heart where I need to surrender to You or get a new perspective. I want You to put me back together. And if there is a way to save this marriage, I am open to Your leading. In Jesus' name, amen.

The Terror of Death

*Do not be afraid of sudden terror or of the ruin of the wicked,
when it comes, for the L*ORD *will be your confidence
and will keep your foot from being caught.*
PROVERBS 3:25–26 ESV

My friend got a very unexpected phone call one Friday.

Her daughter had been killed suddenly in a horrific accident on the interstate.

I can't imagine a terror worse than that.

These are the possibilities that paralyze us if we let them. We know they happen. We are not exempt. They could happen to us. The specter of unexpected tragedy looms in our brains, lurking just behind our consciousness. The phone call. The text. The news we don't want to hear.

Centuries ago, Solomon penned the words of Proverbs 3:25–26. They were inspired by God and protected by His power down through time so we could read them today. I'm sure there were different kinds of sudden terrors back then since they didn't have motorized vehicles and other forms of advanced technology. They didn't have to worry about hearing the word *cancer* because they had no way to diagnose it. And families weren't usually separated by the distances that are part of our lives today. But still, illness occurred, accidental death happened, families experienced difficulties and tragedies. They were people like us, living on a fallen earth where things that aren't supposed to happen do happen.

How do we grapple with the possibility of looming terror? Do we manipulate our children into staying close and never trying anything? Live in a state of denial? Abuse chemical substances so that our minds are numb to the panic? Worry ourselves into a constant state of anxiety?

God says we must take hold of the truth. He will be our confidence. He will keep our feet from being caught in the noose of hysteria. We must center our thoughts on His sovereignty and grace and not on our internal sense of foreboding.

My friend has walked through the fire; she misses her daughter terribly. But God has kept her feet from being stuck in a trap of bitterness. He has been and is being her confidence that she can make it through today and tomorrow and the next day. The tears are ongoing, but so is the grace.

Heavenly Father, thank You for being already there in the next minutes of my life. Teach me to rest in Your providence and in Your promises. Your Word says I do not have to live in worry about sudden terror, for You will be there. I ask You to give me peace as I trust. In Jesus' name, amen.

What We Don't Want

*Heaviness in the heart of man maketh
it stoop: but a good word maketh it glad.*
PROVERBS 12:25 KJV

The letter didn't come.

My daughter had been waiting for it, thinking surely it was time to receive notification that she had been qualified to be either valedictorian or salutatorian of her high school graduating class. She had set her heart on it since her freshman year and worked diligently for four years. She was often the last one up on school nights, sitting in the hallway so as not to disturb her sisters in the bedroom, her head bent over a notebook as she studied. She made excellent grades, took extra classes, and looked ahead to the joy of getting that honor.

But the letter never came.

A technicality in the way the honor points were calculated kept her from being a contender for either standing. She was crushed.

I stood outside the door and heard her sobbing. Four years of work and dreams for nothing, it seemed in that moment. She was heartbroken and a little embarrassed. A heavy heart? For sure.

As her mom, I had a difficult role to play. My heart was in agony for her because I knew how hard she'd worked. And I knew it wasn't an issue of arrogance and snobbery; it was a goal that meant a lot to her that she hadn't achieved. But still, my place was to cry with her and then help her find her footing again. I had to help her put this disappointment into perspective—the perspective of life. And I had to encourage her to celebrate the achievements of others and not let it destroy her graduation day. Wow, what an assignment! Being a mom is sometimes one of the toughest jobs on earth!

I'm glad to say that God helped her with this difficult thing, and she emerged a deeper person. It was still sad, very much so, but it was a time of learning that we can accept unexpected, unwanted situations and move on in life. As a mother, I am learning that this kind of circumstance will likely happen in all my children's lives even before they leave home. And when it does, I have the opportunity to help them approach it biblically and rationally.

I don't know what you face today. Maybe it's something you don't want. Maybe it's something devastating. Maybe not. We really can't compare pain—if it hurts, it hurts. But we can reach out to the same Father who says that even the fall of a little bird catches His attention! That's one of the best comforts ever for our disappointments, big and small.

Father God, thank You for always noticing what is going on in my life. Today I bring to You this disappointment. Guide me as I grapple with it and move forward in spite of it. I love You. Amen.

A Vile Diagnosis

*We await a Savior, the Lord Jesus Christ, who will transform
our lowly body to be like his glorious body.*
PHILIPPIANS 3:20–21 ESV

I like the old King James English wording for Philippians 3:21: "our vile body." At times, I have felt like the apostle Paul must have felt when he wrote that down. He wrote this epistle, this letter to the church at Philippi, perhaps while chained in a Roman dungeon. He had little comfort in that dim, dank place and no doubt suffered not only from the chill but also from illness of some kind or other. Being in an environment with virtually no hygiene, bacteria everywhere, and the presence of sickness in other cells must have combined to make him susceptible to all kinds of sickness. In addition, he was aging and was dealing with the inconveniences that naturally occur with age. When the body begins to break down, we feel betrayed by our own humanity. And we realize how much we long for that better place Christ is going to prepare for us.

I received an unwanted diagnosis as a young adult. Over the years, the disease has ebbed and flowed, sometimes better, sometimes worse. I forget that not everyone deals with the kind of complications that have been part of my life for years. Yet, at some point, if we live very long, all of us will deal with some sort of physical ailment. Our bodies, originally designed by God to live forever, are now contaminated by the cellular destruction of sin at work in our world. They perform valiantly for many years but cannot withstand the principle of death that God promised Adam and Eve would result from their disobedience.

Diagnoses come in every kind of disease imaginable and

unimaginable: cancer, genetic abnormality, cardiac event, neurological disorder, diabetes, dementia, arthritis, fibromyalgia, hearing loss, vision impairment, and so forth. They come in every age bracket and on every continent. They are the reminders that we will not stay on this earth forever. They are shocking, terrifying, life altering, numbing. And they are usually unexpected.

What we do with the diagnosis reveals where our treasure is. Initially, we grieve, because the diagnosis makes us remember that our world is cursed, and we must pay that price. But ultimately, we can trust that our Father is sovereign and if we are *in* Him through faith in Christ, every pronouncement on earth is only part of the plan that heaven is working through. We will struggle with our emotions—we can't trust them. We will be frustrated with our bodies—they aren't dependable. But we will look to our God who is unchanging and yet will one day transform us so that we will be like Him.

Father, give me grace to accept the unwanted diagnosis and let me remember that You will make all things new, and that includes me. Until then, I go on in Your strength. Amen.

A Cracked Mirror

So God created man in his own image, in the image
of God he created him; male and female he
created them. And God blessed them.
GENESIS 1:27–28 ESV

She was the most beautiful maiden in the land. He was brave and strong. They lived happily ever after.

These are our fairy tales. And our dreams. And our expectations.

I don't know about your life, but sometimes the conflict between my husband and me takes me by surprise. Oh sure, there are those days when you know something is going to happen because you're both tired or you've been on a trip or your hormones are super intense. But at other times, conflict just knocks the wind out of you. Why is that?

We all go into marriage with ideals. But most of us know deep inside that the other person is very human. Nevertheless, we're hoping, just maybe, he won't be as human as everybody says he will be. Then we discover that he is. And the image of marriage we see in the mirror has cracks. There's nothing quite like an unexpected fight to remind you of that.

It can be about anything. Or about almost nothing—those are the worst kind. You find yourself defending a position that you really don't even care about. What's worse is that you feel slighted, insignificant, and bulldozed in the conversation.

The important thing to remember in marital conflict is that you are not each other's enemy. But you do have an enemy. It is Satan, who comes as an angel of light, and underneath is a horrible demon. His diabolical tactic in marriage is to deceive each spouse into thinking that the other is against them, when the truth is that he is out to get them both. The suddenness of his attack is breathtaking. And you begin to see in a twisted light the very person you used to behold with such delight.

Thwart the evil blitz of the enemy by focusing on what is true. God created man and woman. God blessed them as a couple. Satan divides. God unites.

Fight for your marriage. Fight for your friend's marriage. Fight for marriage as an institution of God and the basic unit of society. Yes, our earthly marriages are only cracked reflections of what God created. But they can still show His glory in spite of the cracks. The next time the enemy shows up and tries to derail you, remember what's at stake. And fight.

Lord, please help me remember that You created and ordained marriage and that You will help me fight for mine. I want to reflect You even in the cracks that come with life. In Jesus' name, amen.

A Pink Slip

*I have been young, and now am old; yet have I not seen the
righteous forsaken, nor his seed begging bread.*
PSALM 37:25 KJV

Most of us have had the experience of looking for a job. Filling out
applications, submitting résumés, enduring interviews, waiting and more
waiting. Many of us have had the experience of losing a job—either
our own or that of someone else in the family. It's frightening. When a
household loses a major source of income, it can create an imbalance
that is not easily corrected.

I recall a time when both my husband and I were looking for
employment. My husband was a bivocational pastor to a small congregation, and his primary calling and skill set could not provide the
income we needed for a family of six, so he searched for additional work.
Transitioning from homeschool mom to the workplace again while my
four children were in school during the day was a big change for me.
And since I couldn't use my music education degree at the time and
my writing contracts were sporadic, I was also put into the challenging
position of looking for work outside my usual realm. We spent some
anxious days. Some tight days. My husband landed a temporary second
job and then lost it in a few weeks when the weather changed and his
position wasn't needed.

God provided. A man in our congregation suddenly began giving
us gas cards. A few times we received checks in the mail that carried us
through. Once, when we had no money for groceries in a certain week,
my husband worked as a counselor at a local camp for traumatized
children and the kitchen gave him the unserved food from the week.

Did we have everything we wanted? No. We did without some things. But we made it with God's help. When the psalmist wrote this verse, he wasn't meaning that God's people would never be without some things they wanted. He was trying to get us to understand that those who trust in the Lord don't resort to begging, because that implies no one cares for us. We know we are not forsaken. God's eyes are always on the righteous and His ears are open to their cries (Psalm 34:15).

The unwelcome surprise of job loss comes to most of us at some time. And the fears that accompany it threaten us to panic. But remember this ancient text and expect God to act. He will not forsake you, and He will help you get through.

Father in heaven, thank You for always seeing me. I ask for grace to focus on Your provision and for grace to trust You more. Amen.

Seeing You Suffer

The official said to him, "Sir, come down before my child dies."
JOHN 4:49 ESV

Children are supposed to be healthy. They are supposed to outlive their parents. They are supposed to run and play and laugh and have no worries. But things often are not how they are supposed to be.

Pediatric hospitals, for all their bright colors and fun activities, are among the saddest places on earth. There is something intrinsically wrong with weak, wan children. A children's hospital is an oxymoron that will break your heart. The world of needles and tubes, harsh lights, and machines screams at us that something is wrong with our planet, something is terribly broken.

One of the most excruciating things to experience is the suffering of a child, your child. I remember the suddenness of the time when we discovered one of my daughters had a problem with her eyes. She didn't just need glasses; something neurological was going on. A crushing weight of fear descended on my heart, for moms know instinctively when something is wrong. I had a pediatrician tell me years ago, "I always listen to moms; they see things I don't." He was right. I tried to tell myself that this might not be anything much, but I knew better.

If you've ever waited for the results of medical tests, you know both the anticipation and the dread of that wait. And when a diagnosis is confirmed positive, you grieve. Life takes on a different shape.

Some diagnoses are more shattering than others. Some are terminal. Some parents watch their tiny offspring agonize through treatments and get weaker and then breathe a final time. I doubt there can be any greater pain. We would rather suffer ourselves than see our children suffer.

This is something the Father in heaven understands. He watched His Son suffer horribly. He saw Him writhe on the cross and struggle to breathe and then die. As the eternal Son, Jesus chose to die, yes. The Bible tells us that He "gave up" His spirit. But there was no less pain in that for the Father. Maybe there was more. He had a choice. In our children's suffering, we do not.

God walks the halls of children's hospitals. He hovers over the beds of infants and keeps watch on the sleepless nights of frightened little patients. He draws near to suffering parents and hears their crying. One day there will be no more positive diagnoses. One day the curse will be gone forever. One day He will make all things new.

Until then, God beckons us to come close to Him, to remember that He too has suffered, to bring our unexpected agonies to His grace. Like the father who came to Jesus, we come knowing that God has what we need. It may not be healing today, but it will be healing; of that we can be sure.

Father in heaven, today I bring You the grief of suffering children and suffering parents. Today I bring You the things I don't understand, the things that cause such pain. Give me healing in my heart, and Lord, I trust You to make all things new someday. Amen.

Every Little Detail

If riches increase, set not your heart upon them.
PSALM 62:10 KJV

We've all heard the saying "Don't count your chickens before they hatch."

Turns out, that old wise saying is one we should take to heart. If there is anything that can happen unexpectedly, it's money trouble. Everything can be fine, and then *wham*, the bottom drops out. Black Tuesday in 1929 was just such a day—the stock market completely collapsed. The economic effects of the attacks on September 11, 2001, followed that unexpected, blue-skied Tuesday morning. Individual family financial trouble often arrives without notice—the car breaks down, the washing machine stops, a medical crisis occurs, a husband or wife loses a job. Without warning, we are in emergency mode.

When you think about it, money is actually just a symbol of something to which we give value. The metal and fabric of our coins isn't worth anything except the symbolic worth attached to it by our government. Natives of undeveloped areas would have no knowledge that a hundred-dollar bill would be fought over if found on a street in New York City. Currency from other time periods has value because of its historicity, not because it's worth an actual amount today. It's all related to what the symbol represents.

Our money today represents the worth of the gold in our treasury. Other nations have similar systems. Because the treasury holds something in its possession that has recognized value, it can assign a degree of worth to pieces of paper. But what if the gold disappears? The paper is worthless.

Sudden financial distress reminds us that earthly riches are unstable. The writer of Psalms said we should not set our hearts on them. Jesus said in His Sermon on the Mount, "Do not lay up for yourselves treasures on earth, where moth and rust destroy and where thieves break in and steal; but lay up for yourselves treasures in heaven, where neither moth nor rust destroys and where thieves do not break in and steal. For where your treasure is, there your heart will be also" (Matthew 6:19–21 NKJV).

When trouble comes and money gets low and the bank accounts look skinny, we have to remember that our security is not in that, but in Christ. Whether our nation or our families flourish or lag economically, He is the source of our stability. He is able, out of His great riches, to supply what we need today and every day. After all, that's what He'll be doing for eternity for those who love Him—taking care of every little detail. We can trust Him to do that for us today too.

Lord, I proclaim that You are Master of my life and my money. Today I have unexpected financial needs. I bring them to You and trust that You can take care of every detail. In Jesus' name, amen.

Be a Rescuer

Whoever has this world's goods, and sees his brother in need, and shuts up his heart from him, how does the love of God abide in him?

1 John 3:17 nkjv

I have a picture stamped on my brain of my mother standing in the rain before the raised hood of our old white Chrysler, not knowing why it suddenly stopped, and a heroic gentleman coming to our rescue.

When I was a child, my family drove old cars. We were not a wealthy family. Wait a minute. Yes, we were, extremely wealthy, but not in cars. Or in other gadgets and stuff. Our wealth was measured by our family dinnertime and our family worship in church. But, you understand, this kind of wealth does not enable one to drive a new car off the lot. So, we drove older cars, and my father could fix just about anything that went wrong with them. As a child, I remember being a bit chagrined about the fact that our family didn't have the cool kind of vehicles others did, but it was usually a fleeting worry. My life was too wonderful on other accounts for that to bother me for very long. You see, love and loyalty and commitment to Christ in a family have an incredible balancing effect. I was so rich that, to this day, I am amazed at the mass of it.

Still, this particular day, a school morning, found us stalled in the road. Yes, in the road. My mother was a strong, capable woman, but she was not a mechanic. And so, when the man from the auto parts store stepped over to give us a hand, I can imagine her relief. These were the days long before cell phones, and it would have been quite a process to get in touch with my father at his factory job and then wait for him to help us.

Today you may be the one who can offer rescue. The emergency may not be a mechanical issue; maybe it will be a forgotten credit card as someone stands in line to pay for coffee; maybe it will be a misplaced folder for class with study notes for the exam. Maybe you can offer an umbrella in a sudden shower; maybe you can give a water bottle to a sweaty road worker; maybe you can pick up a dropped article for a young mom hanging on to a baby and toddlers. Whatever it is, when the unexpected moment arrives and you have the ability to help, don't shut up your heart. Show the love of God by offering rescue.

Jesus, thank You for being my Rescuer. You came to my aid when You didn't have to. You saw my need and showed me Your love. Help me to do that for others today in Your name. Amen.

God of the Unexpected

Then Martha, as soon as she heard that Jesus was coming,
went and met Him, but Mary was sitting in the house.
Now Martha said to Jesus, "Lord, if You had been
here, my brother would not have died."
JOHN 11:20–21 NKJV

When my youngest brother almost died following a motorcycle accident, he suffered a traumatic brain injury as well as an open-book pelvic fracture. He wasn't breathing when he was discovered beside a utility pole. He had massive internal blood loss. He hovered between life and death in the days immediately following. God chose to spare his life. Martha, however, watched her brother die.

Was Lazarus a sickly person all his life? I tend to think maybe he was, but of course I have no way to prove that. I wonder if this is why he was still living with his sisters and not married with his own family. Perhaps he had a disease that kept him from being able to live a typical life and provide for a family of his own. Living in those times was hard, and a man had to be tough physically just to keep food on the table. Maybe Lazarus had never been able to do that. At any rate, he became very ill. His condition got worse. His disease flared. Or perhaps he was struck by some unexpected illness. His sisters sent word to Jesus, their Friend. They knew He'd want to know. They thought He'd come to help.

But Jesus didn't come right away. And Lazarus died. How could this happen when the family was close friends with God's Son?

Finally, they heard that Jesus was coming. Mary couldn't stop crying in the house. But Martha, the firstborn, couldn't wait. She went out to meet Him, and she voiced her anguish. "If You had just come,

You could have stopped this."

Perhaps today you have been blindsided by a family tragedy. And you know Jesus, so you expect that He will fix it. Maybe you have been surprised by His response. He hasn't done what you thought He should. My thoughts go to the words of C. S. Lewis as he described Aslan, his allegorical symbol of Christ, as "not a tame Lion." God does the unexpected.

Who expected Messiah in a cow's crib? Or angels heralding shepherds? Or the Life-giver hanging on a cross? The empty tomb on a chilly morning? These are the unexpected imprints of our God, His signature in our world. If He can do this, we can trust Him. His response to your need may surprise you, but so will His grace. And someday you'll see a plan so exquisite it will take your breath away.

Heavenly Father, You work in unexpected ways. You see my unexpected tears, and You respond to them according to Your great plan. I trust You today. In the name of Your Son I pray. Amen.

UNEXPECTED FRIENDSHIP

Surprised by Friendship

A man who has friends must himself be friendly.
PROVERBS 18:24 NKJV

We were a contrasting pair. I was a nineteen-year-old newlywed. She was married to a preacher and had kids. I was white. She was African American. I didn't contribute much as the receptionist. She ran needed reports and kept records in the office. But Debbie and I became good friends.

In the print shop where I worked during my first year of marriage, before my husband and I returned to college together, I was young and naive and unused to the language and attitudes around me. There was something gentle and good about Debbie when I interacted with her. We started talking a bit. Then one day we went to lunch together and discovered we both had a weakness for take-out peach cobbler from a local deli. We talked through many a life crisis over Styrofoam bowls of cobbler! She shared the challenges of her life with kids and in ministry. I talked about my anxieties as a new bride and my dreams for the future. And we prayed together. We drew strength from each other in an environment that was sometimes difficult for us both. When I left that job to move to another state, I hated to leave that friendship. I've wondered about her down through the years. Maybe someday we'll see each other again.

Friendship is a part of healthy living. We can live isolated lives, but we won't be emotionally healthy (despite the rhetoric of the mountain men!). God made us for relationship and community. We need interaction with others.

All of us would prefer that people come to us. It's so much easier to make friends when someone else does the hard part of making the first move. But life doesn't go that way. And those who wait around for someone to come to them often keep waiting for a lifetime. This doesn't mean that we should shove our way into people's lives. But it does mean that we can take responsibility for making friendship opportunities. Through our smiles and words, we can invite others to get to know us. I have tried to make this my approach as an older pastor's wife when I attend church events and see someone I don't know. I want to create that bridge to relationship so that others will find it easy to walk across. Some of them will be casual acquaintances and we'll speak to each other and enjoy light camaraderie. Others, though, will become deep friends for life.

Today, keep your eyes and heart open for opportunities to be friendly. Don't wait around. You just might be surprised by the blessing you get out of it.

Dear God, thank You for creating the idea of relationship. You exist in eternal relationship as a triune God—Father, Son, and Spirit. You want us to be friendly with those You put in our lives. Help me do that today. In Jesus' name, amen.

A Friend Who Irritates

Do not rejoice when your enemy falls,
and do not let your heart be glad when he stumbles.
PROVERBS 24:17 NKJV

Do you have an antagonist friend?

You know, it's that friend who gets under your skin every time you interact. You have some things in common and you can talk about the weather and the kids, but it doesn't take long for irritation to rise up when you get past the trivial. There is just something about the way she holds her head or says her words or almost whines or reveals a faint gloat in her attitude that gets to you every time. You try to hold it together and keep smiling, but truth be told, you're glad when a reason comes up to end the conversation.

Yes, we need those kinds of friends too. And we need to see them as friends. All types of friends are important. Scripture says that even if we have actual enemies, we should not celebrate when something bad happens to them. How much more for people we call friends! We should wish good for them and be happy for the things that are going right in their lives, even if they are the type to talk about it often!

No matter how difficult, we need to try to understand them. If talking to them is already painful, we're usually not very eager to find a way to spend more time with them. But sometimes, when we can hear their hearts and not just see the image they project for the first five minutes, we begin to understand the motivation for their irksome ways. Insecurities and anxieties may be the cause. What appears to be narcissism may be an attempt to appear worthy. Perhaps she was abused as a child or never made to feel significant. Maybe her oddities are something she's never noticed. Often, irritating quirks develop in children who have no adults to help them refine their behavior.

Jesus took time for all people—the clean, the dirty, the legal, the criminal, the wealthy, the poor, the healthy, the ill, the fun to be around, and the shunned. He calls us to do the same. And you may discover that you like that person more than you thought you could. You might be surprised with an unexpected friendship with someone you thought you couldn't stand.

God, it's difficult to be nice to this person I'm thinking of right now. Give me grace to go out of my way to be friendly. Help me to celebrate her good news and pray for her troubles. Show me how to get to know her better so I can understand who she really is. In Jesus' name, amen.

Friends with the King

"You are my friends if you do what I command you."
JOHN 15:14 ESV

The old Joseph Scriven hymn says it best:

What a Friend we have in Jesus, all our sins and griefs to bear!
What a privilege to carry everything to God in prayer!
Oh, what peace we often forfeit,
Oh, what needless pain we bear,
All because we do not carry everything to God in prayer!

What an amazing thought: we can be friends with the Son of God! Of course, as my mother used to remind me, He is a kingly Friend. He's not a buddy, a sidekick. But He is a Friend, the very best kind of Friend. He is a Friend who calls us to a higher standard, to decisive living, to absolute commitment. We cannot be friends with Him and also be friends with those who oppose Him.

Writing to the early Christian churches, the apostle James, the half brother of Jesus, admonished his readers on the important correlation between faith and works, between our righteousness through Christ and our relationships. "Do you not know that friendship with the world is enmity with God? Therefore whoever wishes to be a friend of the world makes himself an enemy of God" (James 4:4 ESV).

What is often called "the world" in the New Testament refers to the system of values that operates in the secular culture, the set of ideals and goals that are then displayed in godless behavior. The Bible says we cannot buddy up with this type of living and still be God's friend.

A man in the Old Testament finally figured this out. Abraham was called from a pagan culture in Ur to follow an unknown God so that he could become the father of a great nation that would bless the world. Abraham started out, but he struggled along the way. This was before the atoning work of Christ and the presence of the Holy Spirit. This was even before the Ten Commandments and the Law had been given. Abraham straggled at times, taking detours in his journey, lying about his wife, accepting "help" from Hagar to try to acquire the child of promise, and more. But he corrected his wrong moves, accepted God's help and pardon, and kept moving. And the great faith chapter in Hebrews 11 remembers him as a man of faith. In fact, James had this to say: " 'Abraham believed God, and it was counted to him as righteousness'—and he was called a friend of God" (James 2:23 ESV).

Lord Jesus, thank You for making the way for me to be reconciled to the Father. I am so glad I can be Your friend through the power of the Holy Spirit at work in me. Help me today as I make choices that affirm my friendship with You. Amen.

Used to Be a Friend

*And Samson's wife was given to his companion,
who had been his best man.*
JUDGES 14:20 ESV

"With friends like that, who needs enemies?" an old saying goes.

I think Samson could identify. Yes, he had it coming because he was a jerk. I mean, he found a girl among God's enemies and demanded that his parents get her for him to marry. His parents tried to talk him out of it, to get him to see that he should choose a wife from among those who had faith in God, but he wouldn't have it! So, in some ways, it seems just that his wife was given in marriage to his best man. But still, that had to be a cruel form of betrayal even for a headstrong, unreasonable kind of man like Samson.

Again, we have to remember that we are discussing a story in the Old Testament when they had God's laws but not the power of the Holy Spirit to keep them. They did not have the understanding we have today or even a Bible to read. Scripture often records what happened but does not approve of it. This is one of those times.

Maybe you have had something happen in your life that is a little like what happened to Samson. Maybe you didn't contribute to the trouble like he did. Maybe, just out of the blue, you were betrayed by someone you thought was a friend. Nowhere is this more painful than in the breakup of a marriage. We know the stories of the "other woman" being the best friend of the wife, or maybe it's the husband whose best friend becomes involved with his wife. Like Samson, you are shocked, angered, humiliated. And maybe you feel like doing what he did when he discovered what had happened. Judges 15 says he caught three hundred foxes and tied them tail to tail, attached torches to their tails, and let them run through the fields and orchards of the Philistines, his ex-wife's people. Wow!

But remember, we are called by Jesus to love our enemies. This doesn't mean, of course, that we must conjure up warm fuzzies for a person who has damaged a marriage or has hurt us in some other destructive way, but it does mean that we "love" them by not enacting vengeance on them ourselves. We are not to make them pay. God will do that. And He has much better ways to keep track of what's going on.

When a friend unexpectedly acts in an unfriendly way, the hurt is real. In those moments, we must rely on the strength of our God who never betrays and whose steady love can uphold us in any surprise.

Father God, I've been hurt by someone who was supposed to be my friend. I need Your grace so that I can forgive and not seek vengeance. I ask for strength and peace and hope. In Jesus' name, amen.

The Response of Friends

*Make no friendship with a man given to anger,
nor go with a wrathful man, lest you learn his
ways and entangle yourself in a snare.*
PROVERBS 22:24–25 ESV

You will become like the friends you have. And that is why we caution our children not to develop friendships with those who have traits that are un-Christlike. We want them to become more like Him, not less.

But what about those traits in our adult friends that unexpectedly show up? What do we do about that?

The Bible cautions us about the company we keep. First Corinthians 15:33 (ESV) says, "Bad company ruins good morals." We can't keep hanging around the rebels in life and expect to be different from them.

But at the same time, the Bible tells us that a friend loves at all times (Proverbs 17:17). We are not to be like those who flock around when times are good and disappear when things go bad. A true friend loves even when you've done something wrong.

So how do we respond?

Psalm 1:1 warns us about listening to the counsel of the wicked and lounging around with sinners and relaxing with scoffers. These are the people whose bad ways will corrupt us. However, the Bible doesn't say we can't be a friend to them in the sense of caring about them, talking to them, and trying to love them back to what's right. The problem comes when we make them our confidants and advisers. God wants us to try to help them in the right way.

In fact, Proverbs 27:6 (KJV) reminds us that "faithful are the wounds of a friend; but the kisses of an enemy are deceitful." A real friend will speak up when something's not right.

When your friend unexpectedly shows anger or a bad attitude, you don't have to drop her. But you do need to consider what your response should be. Admittedly, it is difficult if that friend is also a believer. We tend to be defensive of someone criticizing our actions, thinking that is being judgmental. And, well, it is. But that's okay. Jesus told us to use "righteous judgment," not the kind based on appearance (John 7:24 NKJV).

We wish our friends would always react in a way we like. And I'm sure they think the same about us. But when the unexpected happens, you can be prepared to pray and love. And you just might see them change.

Lord, I want to have the right kind of friends influencing me. Help me to use discernment in who I allow to be my closest friends. And help me know how to be a true friend when someone surprises me with an attitude or action that is not like You. I'm depending on Your Holy Spirit for guidance. In Jesus' name, amen.

Heavenly Friends

Do not forget to entertain strangers, for by so doing
some have unwittingly entertained angels.
HEBREWS 13:2 NKJV

It's been a favored theme of authors and screenwriters for centuries—the heavenly being who steps in to assist the beleaguered main character. From Dickens's Ghost of Marley to Frank Capra's Clarence in *It's a Wonderful Life*, angels have been a great addition to the plot. While not all of these angelic friends have traits that are authentically biblical, the Bible does remind us that sometimes strangers are really God's messengers. We are commanded by the inspired writer to show them hospitality.

Few of us imagine that we have made friends with an angel, but it seems to be possible. The way God works in our world is mysterious and known fully only to Him. There are times when it seems we see evidence of supernatural help or protection, and we've heard the stories of those who heard a voice or saw a hand pointing or in some other way were assisted by an otherworldly friend.

Most of the time, God uses what is already in place in our lives to work out His will. But occasionally we might be surprised if we realized just what was happening.

With the increasing lack of true biblical understanding and the growing reliance on personal interpretation as truth, people today often attribute unexplainable events to angels and even call diseased loved ones "my angel." However, we know that God's messengers only do things consistent with God's character and Word. Moreover, our dear departed do not become angelic but rather go either to a place of comfort or torment, depending on whether they accepted or rejected Christ when they were on earth. Still, we must acknowledge this verse that says that angels do show up at times on our earth.

I am not encouraging you to become mystic. But I am reminding you that God has His hosts ready at a second's notice if He wills to use them in your life. You are never out of His thoughts or His reach. Someday He might send a heavenly helper to aid you in a moment of crisis, and if He does, it will be Him working out His plan for you out of His love. No one is more present in our unexpected moments than our great God, who "makes his angels spirits, and his servants flames of fire" (Hebrews 1:7 NIV).

~~~

Heavenly Father, You are the commander of the hosts of heaven. Thank You for sending them to earth when You have a task for them to complete. I may never realize I have seen one of them, but I know I can trust You if ever I need the assistance of a heavenly friend. Amen.

Even in the Bad Times

A friend loves at all times.
PROVERBS 17:17 NKJV

"Fair-weather friends" we call them. These are the kind who are hard to find when the party is over and the cleanup begins. They're nice while they last, but you can't depend on them. You're never really sure if they'll be around or not. And, in fact, it's probably not accurate even to call them friends. They're just acquaintances.

A real friend doesn't just like what's happening around you; she likes *you*. She has committed to investing in the relationship whether you're serving steak or hot dogs. She comes to see you even if your laundry isn't done and your kitchen needs to be mopped and your windows are smudgy. She puts up with your bad moods and your flaws and your weird little ways. She talks you off the ledge during a crisis and brings you coffee on a Monday. She's there to stay.

You know you have one of these friends when the doorbell rings and she stands there and says, "What can I do?" Thanks to the Lord for friends like these!

But we are blessed so that we can, in turn, bless others. We are to be that kind of unexpected, exceptional friend to our friends.

In Luke 11:5–8 Jesus told the story of a man who needs that kind of friend. This man has company show up late at night, and what is worse is that he doesn't have food to offer the guest. What does he do? He thinks of his friend and hops on over to his house and wakes him up. We aren't told if he throws pebbles at the side of the house, calls out, or knocks, but he does something to let his friend know he's there.

The friend isn't very happy, actually. Basically, he says, "Go away;

we've already closed everything up and put the kids to bed. I'm tired."

Well, maybe he wouldn't win the Best Friend of the Year Award! But the other guy persists. And so finally the man in bed gets up and gives him the snacks he needs.

We need to be the kind of friends who get up at the first knock. The kind who love at *all* times—even the sleepy times.

Today you may have the chance to be that kind of friend to someone. It will probably surprise them. They won't expect it. And that will make it all the sweeter.

God, I want to be a friend at all times. Give me the loyalty and the grit to stick with my friends in the hard times, the inconvenient times, the embarrassing times, and the unpleasant times. I know You have all the grace I need to do it. In Jesus' name, amen.

Sacred, Surprising Sacrifice

Greater love hath no man than this,
that a man lay down his life for his friends.
JOHN 15:13 KJV

John 15:13 is often quoted in battlefield stories—a soldier sacrifices his life to save his buddies. It's a verse that speaks to something deep within us, that part of our hearts that resonates with loyalty and love.

One of the ways we might see this verse played out today is in the relationship of pets to their owners. Animals develop lasting bonds of affection for their owners and sometimes display that in amazing ways. A dog may attack a person mistreating its master or even jump into harm's way to save the human it loves.

The classic story *Where the Red Fern Grows* brings us to tears with its recounting of a pair of coonhounds whose hunting days are ended when Old Dan is fatally injured protecting his boy from a mountain lion. The children's tale *Old Yeller* recounts how a mongrel dog earns the love of a family and then is infected with rabies while trying to protect boys in danger. These narratives remind us of the power of sacrificial love and of how a surprising act of devotion moves us to our very core.

Of course, Jesus is the very best image of sacrificial love. He had to *give up* His life. It couldn't be *taken*. In John 10:18 (NKJV), Christ said, "No one takes [My life] from Me, but I lay it down of Myself. I have power to lay it down, and I have power to take it again. This command I have received from My Father."

The whole excruciating ordeal of the scourging, carrying of the cross, the crown of thorns, the nails, and the hours of agony was something Jesus chose to go through. He willingly laid down His life for us.

You might not have the opportunity to physically die for a friend today, but you might have the option to die in some other way. When we refuse to stick up for our rights, we are dying a small death. When we let others choose, we are dying a small death. When we swallow a retort or a sarcasm, we are dying a small death. We can show love by following our Lord's example and denying self.

Jesus, thank You for laying down Your life for me. Today I ask You to empower me to deny myself and love others sacrificially. Amen.

Sweet Coffee Surprise

The sweetness of a friend comes from his earnest counsel.
PROVERBS 27:9 ESV

I'm convinced that some of the popularity of coffee shops is the promise of conversation to which they allude. Somehow, hidden in the marketing is perhaps the subliminal message *If you drink our coffee, you will have great relationships.*

Most of us value friendship. And what better way to talk to a friend than over a fragrant cup of coffee?

I've had a few coffee shop meetings about which I wasn't sure. Maybe I was meeting someone whom I didn't know very well. Maybe I was meeting to discuss a delicate topic. Maybe I was just in a rush that day and didn't want to take the time for a coffee chat. But many times I've been surprised by the blessing of those meetings. Taking time to get to know someone better is an investment, but it usually rewards more than it requires.

The proverb writer is correct: great counsel from a friend is a sweet gift.

I remember the days before coffee became a social phenomenon. People drank coffee, of course, but it was not a life event when they did. They didn't take pictures of their coffee mugs, stand in line for coffee, plan their shopping trips around coffee shops, and all the other things we do today. There were collectible coffee mugs, but they were usually just screen-printed ones from the local restaurant or souvenir ones from vacation spots. There was coffee to buy in the grocery stores but not all the glamorous flavors on the shelves today and certainly not in so many different forms. Grandma and Grandpa drank plain old coffee, probably with a little milk. Restaurants served basic brew with the powdered creamer in packets. But, even then, coffee meant conversation. Friends gathered in kitchens and drank coffee from Corelle cups and talked about life and supported one another and prayed for one another. Coffee was the excuse they needed to gather. And it still is at times.

Maybe you're not a coffee drinker. You can still discover the sweetness of good counsel in friendship. Make the first move. Invite a friend to get iced tea or lemonade with you somewhere and lean into the opportunity to develop your friendship. You never know what unexpected delights you'll discover.

God, every good gift comes from You, and that includes friends and coffee and tea and lemonade. Thank You that I can share these delights with my friends. Amen.

A Ruth Opportunity

Ruth said, "Do not urge me to leave you or to return from following you. For where you go I will go, and where you lodge I will lodge. Your people shall be my people, and your God my God."
RUTH 1:16 ESV

In the category of great relationships, mother-in-law and daughter-in-law are not usually at the top of the list. This is one of those bonds where historically there has been friction—two women loving the same man and wanting to be significant in his affections.

It is a wonderful surprise, then, that God's Word gives us the story of just such a relationship that was close and loving. The book of Ruth is a love story on many levels—the love of Ruth for Naomi, the love of Naomi for her homeland, and the love of Boaz for Ruth. We can learn from all the angles.

If you're married, you know that loving your husband's family is a choice you make, and it takes effort and commitment. Rarely are they like you. They are often from a very different kind of background, eat different foods, use different everyday vernacular, value different kinds of hobbies and celebrations, and may even be from a different culture. That was certainly the case in Ruth's story. Her husband, Mahlon, was a Hebrew, and though his family had been immigrants in Moab for years, no doubt they still retained some of their Jewish preferences. By the time he died, she was aware of most of the differences, I'm sure. Maybe that helped her make her decision. Maybe she thought she knew enough about the land of Israel that she wouldn't have such a difficult adjustment.

Whatever the reason, she begged her mother-in-law not to refuse her request to travel back to Bethlehem with her. Naomi must have been surprised, but the Bible record says that when she saw that Ruth was determined, she gave her consent.

Perhaps you have extended family members who are very different from you. Today, accept Ruth's challenge and look for ways to bond with them in healthy ways. Of course, one should never forsake God for pagan worship or adopt practices that violate His laws. But within those boundaries, why not see how you can surprise them with unexpected overtures of friendship? And who knows? It might open their hearts to Christ if they don't already know Him.

Heavenly Father, thank You for creating different people groups on the earth. You have included some of them in my family. I want to reach out to them and surprise them with friendship that goes beyond mere tolerance. I'm asking for wisdom as I look for those opportunities today. In Jesus' name, amen.

UNEXPECTED ANGER

When the Worms Come

But when dawn came up the next day, God appointed
a worm that attacked the plant, so that it withered.
JONAH 4:7 ESV

I don't like them, but they don't usually make me angry. Worms are a little icky to some of us. Yes, I can bait my own fishing hook, but I don't particularly care for the squishy little things. And I try to avoid stepping on them when they cover the church parking lot after a heavy rain. But I've never had an encounter with a worm like Jonah had. After his triumph of obedience in finally going to Nineveh to preach to the pagan fish worshippers there, the prophet of God had a spiritual battle over a plant and a worm.

Jonah must have felt sure that God would destroy the evil inhabitants of Nineveh. He was, at last, willing to preach to them, but he must not have expected God to forgive them and avert His judgment. This, in Jonah's mind, seemed unjust. And so he sat a distance away from the city and waited to see what would happen.

God allowed a plant to grow up as shade over Jonah's little shelter to give him relief from the heat. And then, just after he was comfortable, God sent a worm to nibble away at the green leaves and destroy the plant. Then He sent a strong, scorching wind that pummeled the prophet in addition to the blistering heat of the sun. And Jonah prayed to die.

It's interesting, isn't it, that the man who ran from God and almost died without wanting to was now asking for that very thing. But God knew that the real problem was Jonah's lack of submission to anything other than what he thought should happen—the call to go to a place he didn't like, the pardon of people he wanted to be judged, the death of a plant that he liked for comfort. He wanted his way. And when he didn't get it, he was angry.

"But God said to Jonah, 'Do you do well to be angry for the plant?' And he said, 'Yes, I do well to be angry, angry enough to die' " (Jonah 4:9 ESV).

What makes you suddenly angry? Is it when something happens that goes against your "plans"? Is it the unexpected event that doesn't match your ideas of God and life? Is it a small thing like a worm eating a plant?

We don't know if Jonah changed his attitude. The Bible narrative ends with God's words to the prophet. But we can write the end of our own narrative today. Anger is a response to unmet expectations. It is a normal human emotion. But the way we channel it and manage it tells us if we are being controlled by the Holy Spirit or by our own willful attitudes.

Creator God, You made us with the ability to feel a range of emotions, and anger is one of them. Please help me today not to become suddenly angry with the way You choose to do things in my life. I want to be Spirit controlled, not me controlled. In Jesus' name, amen.

The Leader I Chose

For the husband is the head of the wife even as Christ is the head of the church, his body, and is himself its Savior.
Ephesians 5:23 esv

We get angry about submission either because we do not understand the concept or because we have a problem with boundaries. Submission is willing response. It cannot be extracted against one's will; that is subjugation. It can only be given. God has given us the noble privilege of choosing the man to whom we will submit. He lets us choose a leader to follow.

There are different kinds of leaders, and there have been many different leaders in history. Some were good; some were bad. Some manipulated their subjects; some inspired them. Some were selfish; some were selfless.

Adolf Hitler maneuvered his way into power in the upheaval of the 1930s in Germany. His rule became more demanding and tyrannical. He expected absolute devotion from his military, personal protective force, and close political circle. When it was not given, he was vengeful. And, in the end, when things looked bad and his country was in jeopardy, he died to save himself, by his own hand.

Contrast that cowardly kind of authority with the life of Christ, who came not to be served but to serve. He asked human beings to follow Him and deny themselves. He responded to cruelty with silence and to mocking with mercy. He offered a way out to His betrayer when He spoke to Judas at the Last Supper. And, in the end, when things looked bad and those He loved were in jeopardy, He died for them.

This is the kind of leadership to which Christ calls our husbands and to which He asks us to submit. It is a cross-imaged headship. And it is good.

The problem for us many times is that our men do this imperfectly, and we are angry at the marred reflection of God's plan. That, however, is not our problem. We, as wives, are asked only to honor the structure the Creator put in place; it keeps things beautifully balanced if we embrace it. This, of course, is not to suggest that a wife should allow herself or her children to be in actual danger from her husband; this type of situation demands an entirely different response, and one that should include professional help. But, for many of us, it's not abuse, but daily life with its daily irritations that affects us.

Today your husband may cause anger to rise up in you. He may not look like the leader God has called him to be. You must remember that you chose him, and you gave your word to stay with him for better or for worse. When he seems to be wanting to save himself instead of sacrificing for you, take him to God! Ask the Father to avenge you if you have been mistreated. Call on the Lord to convict him and show him how to love you as Christ loves His bride, the church.

God, You created marriage and husband-wife relationships.
Give me the maturity and grace to understand Your
Word and the heart of obedience I need to follow it.
Bless my husband today. In Jesus' name, amen.

Workplace Cooldown

Let all bitterness, wrath, anger, clamor, and evil speaking be put away from you, with all malice. And be kind to one another, tenderhearted, forgiving one another, even as God in Christ forgave you.
EPHESIANS 4:31–32 NKJV

If marriage is one of the easiest environments for irritation, the workplace is a close second. While we technically don't "live" with our coworkers, we do spend a lot of time with them in a boundaried setting. And when we observe other humans at close range, almost anything they routinely do can become an aggravation to us.

What does your coworker do that bothers you?

Put her huge handbag on her desk?

Refuse to silence her flamboyant ringtone?

Stretch out his legs and block your way out of the cubicle?

Wear alcohol-laden perfume?

Stand too close in the assembly line?

Pick his teeth?

Blow his nose rudely?

Tap her long nails on the computer keys?

Tell corny jokes?

Mumble?

Cough?

Cry?

Whatever it is, there will be something to tick us off if we let it. And it always seems to happen on one of "those" mornings when you don't need another thing on your plate. It's a sudden reminder that we live in a flawed world with flawed people.

What can we do?

We can pattern our attitude and reaction after the inspired words of Ephesians. Refuse anger and malice and evil speaking, and choose forgiveness and kindness. In a world where people follow their instincts, we can be different and choose to follow Christ above our natural selves.

Lord, today I bring You my coworker who irritates me. Work in me so that I can have a kind response to the sudden irritation that rises up in me. In Jesus' name, amen.

Decelerating the Rage

He who is slow to anger is better than the mighty,
and he who rules his spirit than he who takes a city.
Proverbs 16:32 NKJV

I am not given to loud outbursts while driving. But one day while driving somewhere with my teenage daughter (and probably trying to hurry), the Holy Spirit convicted me of my muttering about the car ahead of me. He seemed to whisper that I was not really modeling Christian grace to my teen who is still picking up cues for her later adult life from me. Of course, I had to agree; the Spirit of God is always right.

Road rage is supposedly a modern complication of our stressful lives. Drivers who are already upset about their day and their obligations and commitments are "driven" to a sudden explosion of anger by a small error or inconsideration on the part of another driver.

I wonder if they had similar problems in Bible times. Most ordinary people didn't own chariots, so it probably wasn't as much of a problem. Animals used to carry things were slow, and everybody knew it. But you can be sure that there were factors that made people feel an emotion similar to road rage. The human psyche can only take so much before it boils over. That's why we need the controlling presence of the Holy Spirit in our everyday lives. When we have surrendered ourselves fully to His work in us, He empowers us to manage these trying situations in a way that doesn't bring harm to others.

Feeling irritation is admittedly a human response to something that isn't just or that hinders our ability to accomplish a goal or that doesn't meet our personal expectations. The emotion itself is clearly just a response. It is the manner in which we express it that becomes either a sin or a grace.

I admit that I often tap my fingers on the wheel when I'm in a hurry and I'm being blocked by other cars, or when I'm waiting at a traffic light. I guess I think that moving something helps a little! But we must be careful not to transfer these bits of impatience into our words and actions toward others.

The wisdom writer says that ruling one's spirit is a greater victory than conquering a city. I think that goes for driving to an appointment without yelling or staring at another driver. God in us wins the victory; our assignment is to give Him control.

Lord, I surrender my driving habits to You. Let me show grace and forbearance toward others, however irritating their driving skills may be. I ask this in Jesus' name, amen.

Weeds of Sudden Anger

"Let both grow together until the harvest, and at the time of harvest I will say to the reapers, 'First gather together the tares and bind them in bundles to burn them, but gather the wheat into my barn.' "
MATTHEW 13:30 NKJV

It's a funny thing, but one of the most common places for sudden anger to occur is in the church. Though it is a sacred setting and we usually associate it with worship, the meetinghouse of believers can also be an environment where people are greatly offended with each other and with the church leaders.

One of the most common criticisms about the church is—you guessed it—the idea of too many hypocrites. You know what? They're right. If there is one hypocrite hanging around and causing trouble, that's too many! These people often give the church a bad name because while their name is *Christian*, which identifies them with other believers, their rotten attitudes and un-Christlike behavior proclaim that they don't really know Christ. When they get mad and gossip, the church is implicated. When they throw a tantrum in the business meeting, children growing up in church remember it. Their anger and malice distort the picture Christians are supposed to present to a hurting world.

There are times when a person must be "put out" of the congregation, but Jesus said not to try to fix all the hypocrites. In this teaching from Matthew 13, He admonished us to let the believers (the wheat) and the fake believers (the tares) exist together in the field (the church). And then during harvest (the judgment), He will sort through the mix.

If you've ever witnessed anger and rage in a church setting, you understand how ironic (and wrong) that is. The place where we come to draw strength from the Prince of peace should not be disrupted by selfish interludes. But draw comfort from the fact that God's eyes miss nothing, and He keeps very good records. Someday all will be set to right.

In the meantime, we must guard our own reactions and examine ourselves to be sure we really are wheat and not shabby look-alike weeds.

Heavenly Father, Your house is to be a place of worship and reverence. Give me grace to keep it that way. Protect my church from the damage of unrighteous anger. In Jesus' name, amen.

Exploding People

In the morning, when the wine had gone out of Nabal,
his wife told him these things, and his heart died
within him, and he became as a stone.
1 SAMUEL 25:37 ESV

Some people have a short fuse, we say. They are especially challenging to figure out. And often they surprise us with their rapid temper.

Abigail was married to just such a man. Nabal, whose name means "fool," was undisciplined and undiscerning. How they came to be married scripture doesn't say. Since arranged marriages were the norm in that time, it is likely that she hadn't had much choice in the matter. Whatever the reason, she was the mistress of a large estate with many animals and servants.

David and his band of men offered volunteer protective service to the landowners and once a year asked for donations of food as a form of payment. Most were happy to help in gratitude for protection from thieves throughout the year. Nabal, however, was surly and impolite to the delegation from David and turned them away empty handed.

David was furious and filled with revenge. He told his men to strap on their swords and prepare for battle. They were going to kill every male in the household of Nabal.

But along the way they were met with a delegation from the other side. It was Abigail, who had heard what had happened and arranged a donation and brought it with her. Her words and her kindness caused David to see that he had been on the brink of committing a terrible sin in God's sight. He took the food and returned to his camp.

Back home, Nabal had been drinking and partying. He didn't know anything about Abigail's trip. The next morning, she told him, and he became so enraged that the Bible says his heart became like a stone. Scripture may be describing a stroke here. His anger actually damaged his body, and ten days later he died.

There isn't a lot of happiness in this story, is there? But there is a lesson. Explosive people will explode. But those of us who are in their lives, however we came to be there, have the opportunity to mitigate some of the damage they do. Of course, we can't take full responsibility for another person's actions, but we can arrange a few "donations" once in a while that might avert something that would hurt all of us.

God, I know an explosive person. To be honest, he [or she] frightens me. I'm asking for Your wisdom to know how to handle those heated situations and for the strength to fill my place in his [or her] life. Amen.

Angry with the Giver

For children are not obligated to save up for their parents,
but parents for their children. I will most gladly
spend and be spent for your souls.
2 Corinthians 12:14–15 esv

Little children don't understand what their parents do. They think their parents are unfair. They don't understand why they must be disciplined. Teens may feel some of the same things. They may articulate it better, but deep down their emotions are similar.

Only when one becomes a parent herself can she begin to understand the weight of parenthood, the inescapable cost of love. The apostle Paul wrote to the Corinthian church about this cost and its relevance to spiritual parenting. Parents are the ones who contribute more to the relationship. They do the saving. And they also do the spending. They exhaust their physical, emotional, financial, and even spiritual resources for the benefit of their children. And the payback is a long time coming. But fathers and mothers spend, not for the return, but for the fact that they want to provide in every way what their children need.

Anger happens when a child relies on his or her immature judgment about Dad and Mom's motives and rules. The child tries to figure out what is happening from his or her frame of reference.

For a parent, the unexpected anger of a child is frustrating and even disturbing. But more than that, the parent has to be attuned to the deeper issue behind the anger. Immaturity is one thing, but an improper concept of authority or a rebellious spirit should not be tolerated.

Father God, thank You for being a perfect heavenly Father. Through Jesus, You spent Yourself completely for me. Let me never doubt Your motives or exhibit a rebellious spirit. I want to be a child who pleases You. In Jesus' name, amen.

Erupting Volcanoes

But the people did not receive him, because his face was set toward Jerusalem. And when his disciples James and John saw it, they said, "Lord, do you want us to tell fire to come down from heaven and consume them?" But he turned and rebuked them.

LUKE 9:53–55 ESV

During His time on earth, Jesus mentored and discipled the twelve men He had chosen to be close followers. He gently exposed their weaknesses and pointed them to the grace of God to help them.

Thomas needed faith. Peter needed restraint. Judas needed integrity. And James and John? They needed mercy.

When the Samaritan village did not receive them, the brothers were incensed. How dare anyone refuse to host Jesus? They wanted to give the townspeople their due, immediately. But Jesus rebuked them and showed mercy. They got a nickname out of it, though. The Gospel of Mark calls them the "Sons of Thunder" (Mark 3:17 ESV).

Maybe we could think of them as being like a volcano, smoldering deep within the fissures of the earth. Then one day, a shift in the landscape, even something minor, causes the right combination of combustion, and the lava spews forth, killing the living things around it.

What character flaw is Jesus refining in your life? Do you have a nickname based on a negative trait you often display? There is no better place to bring your uncontrolled responses than to the power of Jesus. While He will not conquer it for you, He will empower you through His Spirit to make godly choices in your daily life.

The many manifestations of anger boil over and onto others—sarcasm, cynicism, harshness, negativism. At the first bubble of anger, we should turn to Him so it can be defused.

*Lord, thank You for working on me. I'm glad that no temptation
to display selfishness can defeat me if I am abiding in
Christ and choosing in every situation to follow
the direction of the Holy Spirit. Amen.*

UNEXPECTED REST

A Spa for the Senses

He giveth snow like wool: he scattereth the hoarfrost like ashes.
Psalm 147:16 KJV

"Is it snowing?" The question is asked in eager tones by little children.

"Oh no! It's snowing." The statement is groaned out by adults.

The difference in perspective is amazing. And I know that children don't have to deal with the complications that arise from a snowstorm. All they can think of is a day out of school and a fun time playing in the flakes. But what if we looked at a snowstorm as a thing of rest?

Snow slows down the tempo of living. It just does. Traffic moves slower; events are delayed or postponed; plans are changed. It's an opportunity for an interlude of rest.

The Bible says that God gives snow. He *gives* it. Sure, it makes life a little more complex, but maybe it's okay if we just stay in. Maybe gazing across the field at the sea of white with a coffee cup in one hand and a quilt in the other is the kind of soul rest that's needed.

I hear you. Work must go on. There are no excuses for adults. That's true. But maybe after work you can clear your evening and take advantage of the atmosphere gentled around you by the swirling white.

The muffling effect of falling snow helps to tune out the daily noises. The monochromatic silvery tones of the snow and ice give the eyes visual rest from the bright lights and bold colors of marketing. The chill in the air invites burrowing under a plush throw, encouraging the body to relax and be warmed. The aroma of a hot drink beckons the palate and soothes the taste buds. Snow is a full-on spa for the senses.

So the next time the weather report indicates snow is arriving, start getting ready to rest! You might find that you look forward to snow days more than ever before! And I think that would make the Creator happy. He is the Giver, after all.

———⟿———

Creator God, thank You for snow and for the promised interlude of rest. I want to be grateful for the variety of weather You give to the earth. Help me to take advantage of the rest for my senses. Amen.

A Person of Rest

I have calmed and quieted my soul, like a weaned child with its mother; like a weaned child is my soul within me.
PSALM 131:2 ESV

Have you ever met someone who embodied rest, who made you feel calm just being in her presence?

Those people are unusual. I don't think I'm naturally one of them. But I want to learn how to become like them.

I am naturally an intense person, maybe what could be called high-strung. Phlegmatic is not one of my temperament traits. But is it possible to learn to project calm and peace?

The psalmist said that he had "calmed and quieted [his] soul." It sounds like a deliberate action, a choice. A weaned child is one who has learned to be content without mother's milk; he or she has grasped the idea that comfort is still found in the presence of mother though the roles have changed. A weaned child is not fretful and restless but quiet and at rest.

To accomplish this in the spiritual life, one must follow the words of the first verse of the psalm: "O LORD, my heart is not lifted up; my eyes are not raised too high; I do not occupy myself with things too great and too marvelous for me."

The way to soul rest in the Lord is to refuse to get focused on matters that are out of our hands. We must not allow our minds to be occupied with outcomes that only come from God's throne. We must let Him keep the answers to the unsolvable earthly equations. We must not lift up our hearts and imagine that we can sort things out; we must not elevate our eyes to the level where God reigns.

You may get the chance today to provide a moment of rest for someone. Our world is filled with people who are jostled by every kind of stress one can imagine. Maybe an encounter with you, filled with the Holy Spirit, could cause them to consider letting God rule. After all, if He can quiet you so you bring rest to others, He can use that rest to be a witness.

Lord, I'm glad for the promise of rest. Like the psalmist, I want to choose purposefully to be calm and quiet. And I want to bring unexpected rest to others. In Jesus' name, amen.

Doing It Differently

"Moreover, I gave them my Sabbaths, as a sign between me and them, that they might know that I am the LORD who sanctifies them."
EZEKIEL 20:12 ESV

Many people treat Sunday like an extra part of the weekend. Actually, it is the first day of the new week. And it is also a sacred day.

Since Jesus rose on Sunday, the New Testament church began meeting for worship then instead of on Saturday. They took the principle of one day in seven as an interlude of rest and worship and applied it to Sunday. If it is the creative plan still at work (as all other aspects of the creation pattern we still affirm), then it is still a day to be set aside as different from the rest.

In our culture, it is a surprise to find those who practice Sabbath rest. Rather than taking the boat to the lake after church or using it as a travel day for the end of vacation, what if we were serious about setting aside Sunday as a time of actual rest and worship? What if we put some boundaries in place that would help us keep it sacred and holy? What if we surprised those around us with an innovative new approach to less stress—Sundays at church and home!

The Quakers, or Society of Friends, objected to the use of traditional names for the days of the week because of the non-Christian Saxon origin. So they called Sunday "First Day." Not a bad reminder to all of us that it should be first in our minds—a day that sets the rhythm for the rest of the week.

God designed the Sabbath as part of His covenant with His people. Keeping the Sabbath was very important in Jewish law and culture. Indeed, God said through Ezekiel that it was even a sign of their sanctification, or "set-apartness." It would surely be the same for us today. Sabbath or Sunday keeping is a practice that marks those who have a reason to make it different. And indeed, we do have a reason. We know the Creator of the week and the Originator of rest.

This week, do something wildly different. Keep Sunday special, sacred, and restful. Plan your activities for other days. You might just bring a little more rest to this world by someone else you influence.

God, thank You for creating the Sabbath principle for us.
I want to incorporate more rest into my life because I know
it honors You and is healthy for me. I'm glad I can be
purposeful about this important part of my week. Amen.

Listen to the Cues

Return, O my soul, to your rest;
for the LORD has dealt bountifully with you.
PSALM 116:7 ESV

Sickbed rest is forced rest, interrupted rest, unplanned rest. But it is rest.

I used to hear people say that God had to "put someone flat on his back" to get him to rest. Maybe that's just a colloquial way of saying that the person wouldn't rest unless he or she was sick. But I think God sometimes uses illness to get us to rest our bodies.

Moms generally feel that we don't have time to be sick. I remember a season of my life when I was busy working outside my home while my children were in school, and also helping my husband with ministry at the church we were pastoring. I had a long commute every day; it was winter, and the old car we were driving was not properly heated. I wasn't getting enough rest, and I was stressed. I picked up a fever and a cough, and then my lungs started to burn when I was outside. I was diagnosed with pneumonia.

I felt near to hysteria. My oldest hadn't been driving for very long, and now I had to trust her to take her three siblings on an hour-long commute in winter weather to the Christian school they were attending. I was so sick I could barely leave my bed. My body wasn't giving me any choices. I had to rest.

That wasn't the way I had planned things. But God made our bodies to give us cues, and if we ignore those cues, our bodies will simply shut down on us and force us to rest. That's the kind of unexpected rest we don't relish. In fact, most of us dread the winter season when we are crammed indoors and germs float as freely as drifting snowflakes!

But even in forced rest, God is at work. He restores our bodies when they get proper sleep and food and care. And if we pay attention to the cues and take a day off, we might just be around a bit longer!

God, You are the genius behind our amazing bodies. You built into them alarms and cues that tell me when I need to take better care of myself. Help me listen to them so that I can take better care of this temple of the Holy Spirit. In Jesus' name, amen.

You Can Rest Someday

Discipline your son, and he will give you rest;
he will give delight to your heart.
PROVERBS 29:17 ESV

When my children were small, rest was difficult to come by. I was physically tired much of the time, and I'm not sure I thought about the fact that someday emotional rest would be more important to me than bodily rest. But that's what Proverbs promises the faithful parent.

Toddlers are busy little people. They move from one activity to another with lightning speed. And they are smart. They know how to test the limits of moms' boundaries and even rebel against them. It's so important that we meet their questions with answers. In other words, when their actions ask, *Will you keep your word?* we answer yes with whatever consequence is appropriate.

The Bible places on parents the responsibility to guide their children into proper respect for authority. This begins in the early years. A child who learns to obey Mom and Dad will then transfer that to other healthy relationships in school and church and ultimately to God. And the bonus is that children who know there are boundaries in their world are more secure!

God's principles often seem to run counter to the wisdom of the culture. Advice from secular sources may discount strong discipline or even discourage it altogether. But we know that the rules from the One who made us will work.

If we do not discipline our little ones, we will only exchange physical exhaustion for emotional exhaustion as we continually battle disrespect and obstinacy in the teen years and then agonize over their unhealthy life choices and heartbreaking situations when they're adults. The delight of heart that comes from doing the work in the early years will far outweigh the inconvenience!

If you're a mom with little children today, invest in their future and yours by using loving discipline. You won't be sorry.

Father in heaven, thank You for my children. Give me the wisdom and love I need to discipline them today and the stamina to keep faithful day after day. In Jesus' name, amen.

Enjoy the Drive

The heart of man plans his way,
but the LORD establishes his steps.
PROVERBS 16:9 ESV

Ever had your vacay plans changed? The cruise is canceled, the flight is delayed, the destination suffers a disaster, the family gets sick, or a death occurs and the funeral must be attended—all of these things can derail our plans for a fun getaway.

Things take us by surprise, and we have to adjust accordingly. It's part of the way life on earth goes sometimes. We can't predict what will happen when we make the reservations months ahead of time and schedule the week off work. Only God has foreknowledge.

God often is in the changes, though. Not just in a week away but on the larger scale. As we navigate life, detours sometimes take us down different career roads or ministry paths than we had on our personal map. But the God who led Abraham to an unknown land and guided the Hebrews into Canaan is the One who directs our steps. He made a way through the Red Sea and brought them through the wilderness into the land of promise. He surely knows how to lead us through the twists and turns that seem so confusing.

I love to drive on country roads; they're much more interesting than city streets. They wind and bend around ridges and valleys, pass by quaint farmhouses and pastures, and meander through little villages. The delight is that you're on an adventure and never can tell what lies around the next turn.

God's map for our lives is sometimes like that. And we can find joy in trusting Him and hanging on for the ride! I know that we like to know the details and figure out where we're going, but sometimes that just isn't possible. We don't always know how long we'll stay in one location. But He does! And we can know that whenever He brings us to an unexpected crossing, He already knows exactly where we need to go next. And He'll get us there!

Father, I don't know exactly where I'm going in life, but I trust Your leading. I give You my anxious thoughts and fears and desire to control the future. Lead me for Your name's sake. Amen.

Set Your Limits

*We urge you, brothers and sisters. . .to make it your ambition to
lead a quiet life: You should mind your own business and work
with your hands. . .so that your daily life may win the respect of
outsiders and so that you will not be dependent on anybody.*
1 Thessalonians 4:10–12 niv

The charm of Amish life is the appeal to rest.

Each year, tourists flock to Amish settlements in Pennsylvania,
Ohio, and Indiana to observe the quaint way of life in a pastoral setting
and to enjoy delicious food and wholesome entertainment. From the
fry pies to the deli cheese, from livestock auctions to shopping, the
menu and pastimes are meant to point to a slower pace. The unending
publication of Amish novels and even the development of Amish "reality
shows" serve as testament that we can't get enough of this simple life
for which we long.

The Amish are actually a very busy people, but their industriousness
is of a different kind. They put in long days in the fields and kitchens,
plowing fields, planting crops, raising barns, cooking and canning, and
caring for large families. They purposefully avoid some of our technology
that increases the pace of our days.

For many the decision of the bishop not to allow automobiles is
not based on the idea that driving is a sin but on the predication that
motorized vehicles separate families and create greater distances
between them. The restrictions on phone usage, which vary from
congregation to congregation, are to lessen distractions in the home
where family members would be pulled away from the unit. We have
to admit that there is truth behind these principles.

And so, deliberately, intentionally, the Amish create and preserve for themselves a life that is quiet and slow compared to ours. There is certainly nothing wrong in doing so. And it continues to draw the rest of us to their communities to try to soak up a bit of their contentment.

The surprise in today's reading is that purposeful restriction, making intentional restraints in our activities and indulgences, may result in rest. How can you apply this to your own life? Certainly not everyone will lead an Amish life. But almost all of us need to restructure some of the aspects of our too-often frantic lives. What can you limit that will turn around and be a direct blessing in your life? Take a few minutes to think about it.

Lord, I want to lead a quiet and peaceful life in every way I can. Show me how I can be purposeful about eliminating distractions and needless busyness. I know that I cannot be lazy and please You, but neither can I honor You by living without boundaries. Thank You for helping me to see this. Amen.

God Chose to Rest

And on the seventh day God ended His work which He had done, and He rested on the seventh day from all His work which He had done. Then God blessed the seventh day and sanctified it, because in it He rested from all His work which God had created and made.

GENESIS 2:2–3 NKJV

Is there anything more unexpected than the all-powerful, ever-constant Creator taking a break?

That's what the second chapter of Genesis tells us took place on the seventh day of creation. God finished His work with the creation of humankind. And on the seventh day, the Creator rested. He didn't rest because He was tired. The kind of resting He did was a cessation of work; it was a pattern He established for us from the very beginning—a day of rest in the week.

That in itself is intriguing. God lives outside of time and space. But He created time for us, for earth. And He confined Himself to the space of a twenty-four-hour day so that He could show us what kind of rest we should do.

Rest is a biblical theme from the beginning. We see it continued all throughout scripture. It is listed in the fourth commandment given to Moses. It was strictly observed in the nation of Israel, and in Jesus' day, it had become so important to the strict religious leaders that "resting" was almost tiresome with all the extra restrictions. God's intent, however, was that we should have a day to rejuvenate our minds and stop our work. Remember, He instituted a day of rest even before the fall of man and woman, before sin entered our world and twisted the way things work.

Jesus affirmed God's loving plan for rest when He said in Mark 2:27 that the "Sabbath was made for man." It is a gift, made for mankind's good. Hebrews 4 speaks of the importance of the concept of rest—both in a literal sense and in a spiritual, eternal sense.

So don't be surprised that God would rest! Delight in the fact that He provided this pattern for us, and plan it into your week. You can't imagine the rewards you'll get from it.

Dear Father, I need rest, and I thank You for showing me the way to put that into my week. You give us good things, and a day of rest in the week is one of those. Help me to be purposeful in keeping it. In Jesus' name, amen.

Sudden Calm

And he awoke and rebuked the wind and said to the sea, "Peace! Be still!" And the wind ceased, and there was a great calm.
MARK 4:39 ESV

As I get older, I value "calm" more and more. I enjoy silence more than I used to. My teens loved to keep music going or some other type of action happening. But my mom ears, at times, craved the quiet.

To value a calm, you must contrast it with chaos.

For Jesus' disciples, this happened after a day of being with Him while He taught. They let Him take a nap while they rowed the boat to the other side. But, as is common on the Sea of Galilee, a sudden storm arose, violently slapping the boat around and beginning to fill it with water. Imagine the shrill whistle of the winds and the pitching of the little ship. Think about the darkness on the water with only crude oil lamps for light. Picture them bailing out water with wooden buckets and with their hands, terrified they were going down. And Jesus was sleeping on a cushion. Of course they woke Him. Wouldn't we?

He scolded the wind and waves. He told them to calm down. And they did—just like that. Smooth as glass. A tranquil, beautiful evening with moonlit waters. In an instant.

Storms arise in our lives as suddenly as they do on the Galilee. We can go from smooth seas to vicious waves in a phone call or a text message. Everything begins to pitch and roil, and all we can hear is the moan of the winds as Satan tells us that it's really over this time.

I'm so glad we have the One who brings calm. His voice speaks the frequency that nature recognizes. And it also speaks the code that opens our hearts. When He stands up and addresses our chaos, we know peace is on the way.

What is happening in your life today? What storm has kicked up its heels in your family, in your life, in your health, in your relationships? Turn to Him. Listen to His voice. Expect the calmness He can bring to your heart.

~~~

Dear Lord Jesus, You calmed the seas when You were on earth. I need You to calm my heart today. I know that nothing is beyond the power of Your voice, and I trust Your peace. Amen.

UNEXPECTED PAIN

A Fake Love

When the LORD saw that Leah was unloved, He opened her womb;
but Rachel was barren. So Leah conceived and bore a son, and she
called his name Reuben; for she said, "The LORD has surely looked
on my affliction. Now therefore, my husband will love me."
GENESIS 29:31–32 NKJV

When a woman marries, she expects to be happy. Usually. At least in our modern culture. But not so much in biblical times. Arranged marriages were the norm, and romantic feelings were not necessarily part of the equation. But girls knew that was the way things were. Still they had anticipation of a ceremony and then a new home and babies someday.

So, imagine what Leah's wedding day was like. She was married incognito. The man in the ceremony thought she was her sister. And all the affection he showered on her and the sweet things he whispered to her that night were not really hers; they were sentiments for another woman. Can you comprehend how painful that was?

The Bible says that Leah had weak eyes (Genesis 29:17). Maybe she was nearsighted; maybe she was unattractive in some way. Whatever the reason, the verse goes on to say, "But Rachel was beautiful in form and appearance" (ESV). Leah was the negative contrast to her lovely sister.

And after the wedding night, Jacob discovered that he had the wrong woman. "And in the morning, behold, it was Leah!" (Genesis 29:25 ESV). The wording of that verse doesn't sound like it was a welcome discovery. Think of the embarrassment that was for Leah, to see her new husband's eyes widen and his expression change from adoration to shock to maybe recoil. Probably Leah had no say in the deception; she had to follow the will of her father as the custom was. Maybe she was secretly glad that she was getting a desirable husband because her chances weren't good otherwise. Maybe she felt terrible that she was getting the man her sister was pining for. Maybe she hated every minute of a wedding that didn't really belong to her. We don't know.

We do know that she was unloved. The Bible says so. The unexpected pain in Leah's life was that she was used by others and not appreciated as herself. The scripture says that after she had borne her first child, she believed that her husband would love her.

I hope you haven't experienced that kind of pain. But our God sees the pain you do have, and He cares, just like He cared for Leah. I know He wants to help you bear up under the sadness you're carrying. You may not find acceptance and respect from others, but to your Creator, there is no person like you. Bring your story to Him, and you may be surprised by the love you find.

Heavenly Father, I've had unwanted negative reactions from others. I'm afraid to trust, but I bring my story to You and ask You to help me find my balance in You. Thank You for loving me. In Jesus' name, amen.

The Prodigals We Love

*A foolish son is a grief to his father
and bitterness to her who bore him.*
PROVERBS 17:25 ESV

A popular saying goes that being a mother is like forever carrying your heart around outside your body. It's true. Mothers' hearts are made of strong stuff—they have to be. They carry the burdens of their children and never give up. Yet they are also fragile enough to break when the child is rebellious and irresponsible.

One of the most painful, unexpected situations in our lives is the discovery that a child is in trouble through bad, maybe even sinful, life choices. In a moment of time, a son or daughter chooses a path that puts them in a life of regret for years to come—alcohol use, illegal drug consumption, pornography, rash loans, credit card debt, relocation, hasty marriage, sex outside marriage, rejection of faith, not attending church, body-altering procedures.

Some of these have an easier solution than others. Some of them are life scarring. Some have consequences that affect many others. The proverb writer had it right. A foolish child breaks his mother's heart. Why does this happen?

Remember that adult children are their own responsible party. Regardless of whom they would like to blame, ultimately they make their own life decisions. Only those severely mentally or emotionally impaired live off the decisions of others.

Remember that individual temperament can affect the disparity between the choices of one child and those of another. Some are born with rebel spirits. Thus the hard work of teaching submission must be done in the early years. But at times we fail to do so. And some children have such strong wills that God must finally bring them to a crisis to get them to surrender. "Those who will not learn must feel," goes the old saying.

And remember also that God specializes in bringing prodigals home. Don't give up hope on yours.

If you have a young child in your home right now, stay on the job and put into place the framework that will reap the rewards of good choices in the years to come.

*Father in heaven, work in the heart of my "foolish child"
today. Awaken my child to the truth. Help me
love and hope and trust in You. Amen.*

Wounds in the Body

I entreat Euodia and I entreat Syntyche to agree in the Lord.
PHILIPPIANS 4:2 ESV

The jokes about church "bosses" and conflict in the church are sadly often reflective of truth. Anywhere there is a group of people working together, there will be conflict. The question is, how will it be handled and resolved?

Unbelievers fight for their individual way and rights. The "natural man" is more concerned with winning than anything else. But Christians are called to a higher plane, a better way.

Jesus said, "By this all people will know that you are my disciples, if you have love for one another" (John 13:35 ESV).

What marks Christians is not the absence of conflict but the way in which we handle it. The love we have for one another is to outshine our desire to win. In fact, if the desire to have our own way is so dominant, we may need to seriously examine our surrender to the Spirit's control in our lives.

In his letter to the Philippian church, the apostle Paul urged two Christian women to reconcile in the name of Jesus. Any disagreement we have cannot be more important than our ties as sisters in God's family. That is an eternal bond. The things we debate and champion down here will mostly fade away when this earth is dissolved with fervent heat (2 Peter 3:12). But the kingdom of God and the work we do for Him will last.

Perhaps you have been surprised by wounds you received in church, in the place that was supposed to be safe, in the environment where you thought everyone would always agree. Remember that people in the family of God are still works in progress but that Christ never condones unkindness or grudges. Remember that what is most important is how we handle conflict. And remember that love heals wounds.

Father God, Your church, Your body, sometimes experiences divisions. Jesus prayed for believers to be unified in their love for You and for each other. Help me to be part of the solution. And let me respond with kindness when I receive unexpected wounds. In Jesus' name, amen.

The Lob Shots

Likewise, husbands, live with your wives in an understanding
way, showing honor to the woman as the weaker vessel,
since they are heirs with you of the grace of life,
so that your prayers may not be hindered.

1 PETER 3:7 ESV

There is a difference in wives being sensitive and in taking offense. One is feminine design; the other is willful action.

Women are designed differently than men. God decided that two beautiful diverse and complementary genders would best image His eternal being, so He made man and woman. And He gave them different sets of characteristics.

Setting stereotypes is tricky. The men and women who people the earth represent an amazing variety of traits and preferences and gifts. Nevertheless, we can take some cues from the Bible, for it is God's infallible Word and because the Creator inspired its wisdom.

The apostle Peter admonished husbands to live in understanding with their wives and explained that women are the weaker vessels. His words have no doubt given heart palpitations to generations of feminists. But taken in context and with an understanding of God's design, they shouldn't.

Women are physically weaker. Blame it on testosterone, the hormone that makes a human male. We don't have the same degree of it. We're not supposed to. Women are delicate in other ways too. Since we are highly relational in our approach to life, we are more likely to be wounded in relationships. This indicates an emotional sensitivity. That does not make us incompetent or not valuable. It makes us women.

And it is a matter of course that our husbands will be different and will, unintentionally at times, hurt us. They will say things and do things that astound us. We can't imagine how they "don't hear" the way those things sound to us!

In those moments, we have a choice. We can build a wall, start a list, begin a war. Or we can feel the hurt and take it to our burden bearer, Jesus. The Bible says that God will deal with our husbands if they are mistreating us. I don't know how that all works, but I do know that a sincere Christian man won't be able to get very far in his quiet time with God before the Holy Spirit shows him that he needs to correct his wrong against his wife.

Sometimes our husbands need us to communicate honestly and lovingly about the effect of their words because they genuinely don't know. That's okay too. But let's never take those unexpected lob shots and use them as an excuse to be unforgiving women. God can handle these kinds of things.

Lord, You created men and women and know them very well. Thank You for making me a woman with all the gifts and limitations that go with it. Today, help me to use my relational sensitivity in good ways and never to wield it as a weapon. In Jesus' name, amen.

Powerful Fallout

*So put away all malice and all deceit
and hypocrisy and envy and all slander.*
1 PETER 2:1 ESV

Words have weight.

Few words are more powerful than "I love you" or "I hate you." The impact of these words can only be measured by human hearts.

Every day we give and receive words. Every day we are vulnerable to their effect on us. Every day we are open to being wounded.

One of my challenges as a mom is in helping my children deal with the fallout of hurtful words. Sometimes it takes awhile for me to find out about an incident. Preteens and teens seem to have the idea that keeping hurts inside makes them go away. Or they don't want to bring them out in the open and examine them.

In talking with my own children and in discussing these kinds of hurts with others, I have stumbled upon some guidelines:

- Don't believe the words of immature, unstable, angry people.
- Hold to the truth about yourself as a person of significance to God and others.
- Don't try to figure it all out; some things never make sense.
- Forgiveness is not a feeling; it's choosing not to make the other person pay.
- Say aloud, "I forgive you," and forgive as an act of your will, a choice.
- Read God's thoughts about you and surround yourself with people who reflect His love.

God's Word commands us not to engage in slander because it's evil and destructive—a tool of Satan.

Often, hurtful words descend on us unexpectedly. Out of the blue, we say. They are hurled in a conversation, blasted in a text, or posted across social media. But for every single one of them, Jesus has the antidote. His grace in our lives enables us to rise above—and not to respond in kind.

Lord, with Your help, I will refrain from slander today. I want to use my words to uplift and bless. Give me grace when I feel verbally attacked. Help me to respond as Your child. In Jesus' name, amen.

A Different Image

But to Hannah he gave a double portion, because he loved her,
though the LORD had closed her womb. And her rival
used to provoke her grievously to irritate her,
because the LORD had closed her womb.

1 SAMUEL 1:5–6 ESV

Infertility is a pain that blindsides you.

Every woman expects to be able to bear a child. We assume it's just part of the territory. But when it doesn't happen in the normal, God-appointed ways of marital living, a woman begins to feel unnatural, damaged, inadequate, a failure.

Many women in the Bible are described as "barren." The Hebrew word means a destruction of the generative organs. It makes me think of an arid wilderness, a place where life cannot spring forth. It's a withered, lonely description.

Being childless was the worst possible state for a woman in ancient times. People looked down on her for her inability, they pitied her husband who had no heirs, and they knew she was bound for a very difficult life since she had no sons to take care of her in her old age.

Today a woman who grapples with infertility still faces social stigma and crushing personal pain. She finds it hard to believe that she actually is unable to conceive a child.

Hannah's husband loved her and tried to comfort her. He gave her his day's equivalent of roses and special treatment. But his other wife was not so thoughtful. In fact, she used Hannah's pain as a bludgeon, making rude comments and chiding her for her lack. So when Hannah went to the house of the Lord and prayed fervently, this was a very deep moment for her.

The way Hannah's story ended may be different from how your story ends. God did open her womb and give her a son, whom she gave back to God's service. You may not conceive. You may not even be able to adopt. But God sees the pain you carry.

We have expectations for our lives. Infertility mars the image we have in our minds. But it doesn't mar the image God has in His. His plans for you are good and perfectly suited to His will.

Maybe you don't personally struggle with infertility, but you have a friend who does. You have the opportunity to be a blessing to her. Open your heart to the leading of the Holy Spirit and be part of the salve she needs today.

Father, infertility is a result of the curse on our world.
But I know that You can use even that for Your glory and that
You have a different story for each one of Your daughters.
Use me today as an ambassador of hope. Amen.

UNEXPECTED LAUGHTER

Loneliness Turned to Laughter

You have turned for me my mourning into dancing;
you have loosed my sackcloth and clothed me with gladness.
PSALM 30:11 ESV

Loneliness isn't usually a setting for laughter. When we think of laughter, we think of happy gatherings with friends and food and fun; we imagine sharing lighthearted moments with those whose company we enjoy.

The man who wrote Psalm 102 knew what it was to be lonely. "I am like a desert owl of the wilderness, like an owl of the waste places; I lie awake; I am like a lonely sparrow on the housetop" (vv. 6–7 ESV). He used vivid imagery to describe his feelings—an owl in waste places and a lonely sparrow on the housetop. These are not the descriptions of a joyful person. And certainly not the setting in which we expect to find laughter.

Can one laugh alone?

Actually, yes, if you have something to laugh about. Psalm 30, written by David, was used for the dedication of the temple. He exulted about the things the Lord had done for him, how God had come through for him time after time. He praised Him for His mighty deeds and great power.

These are things we can be joyful about even when alone. Celebrating the triumphs of our God is always appropriate—alone or with others. And it can include laughter. The book of Exodus records how Moses and Aaron's sister, Miriam, led the Israelites in a joyous celebration after the Lord brought them through the Red Sea. "Then Miriam the prophetess, the sister of Aaron, took a tambourine in her hand, and all the women went out after her with tambourines and dancing. And Miriam sang to them: 'Sing to the LORD, for he has triumphed gloriously; the horse and his rider he has thrown into the sea' " (15:20–21 ESV).

Our God specializes in turning the negative into positive. If we focus on Him and His power, we can be surprised by the joy He brings to our hearts and the life we feel in our spirits. Circumstances may be the same, but the awareness of our faith in the One who is ever present and all-powerful makes all the difference in the world.

Jehovah God, You are the Great One. You see me in my aloneness. You have rescued me in the past. You will do it again. I trust You, and I choose to laugh aloud because of the victory I know I have in You. Amen.

Laughing with Joy

When the Lord saw her, He had compassion on her and said to her, "Do not weep." Then He came and touched the open coffin, and those who carried him stood still. And He said, "Young man, I say to you, arise." So he who was dead sat up and began to speak. And He presented him to his mother.
LUKE 7:13–15 NKJV

When someone dies unexpectedly, it often feels surreal that he or she is really gone, especially if the person was young and healthy. You'll have moments when you have to remind yourself of the grim reality because it seems like a horrible nightmare from which you will surely awaken. It must have been so for the mother of this man in Luke 7. He was her only son, her pride and joy, as well as her security in her old age. She was a widow, and now no one was left for her.

Have you been there? Maybe at a funeral or maybe in a cemetery of extinct hopes, a place where there is no life, no future. You watched your tomorrows pass before you on a funeral bier. There are all kinds of deaths and all kinds of loss. Yours may feel as agonizing to you as the widow's was to her.

Someone has said that Jesus disrupted all the funerals He ever attended. What a happy fact! As He and His disciples approached the city gate, the funeral procession was leaving. This was common enough. But Jesus was touched by the mother's grief. Perhaps He thought of His mother and His approaching death. Maybe there was some particular characteristic about this death or this mother that moved Him. We do know that Jesus was always filled with compassion for the people around Him, the suffering ones, the sinful ones, the separated ones.

I can imagine Jesus laying a gentle hand on the woman's shoulder as He said, "Don't cry." Maybe she looked up at Him and wondered why He would say that. Then He walked to the coffin, touched it, and spoke to the dead man. And the man sat up and began to talk. I wonder what he said!

I am always thrilled that Jesus speaks to those who are dead as though they can hear. They can. His voice penetrates even the veil of death, and life springs forth when He calls. Imagine the joy, the laughter of that mother and her son, as they walked back home together. Together!

You may be grieving today. Jesus is passing by. Let Him speak comfort to your sorrow and life to your loss. Watch Him work, and hear the laughter as you join the procession that isn't going to the cemetery now!

*Dear Lord Jesus, You are life and peace. I bring to You
the dead hopes of my life and ask You to revive
my spirit with Your power. Amen.*

Laughing with Relief

*"Or what woman, having ten silver coins, if she loses one coin,
does not light a lamp and sweep the house and seek diligently
until she finds it? And when she has found it, she calls together
her friends and neighbors, saying, 'Rejoice with me,
for I have found the coin that I had lost.' "*

LUKE 15:8–9 ESV

Have you ever laughed when you found something? Maybe you found it in an unusual place. Or maybe you were just delighted to see it again! A few times I have been so relieved to be "found" again that I could have laughed if I hadn't felt so weak with relief!

I recall being alone and "lost" in an unfamiliar area on the way to pick up my daughter at a class event. It was held a good distance from our home, and after dropping her off I had gone shopping in a nearby town so that I would be near when the event ended. But I got turned around going back. And to make matters worse, it seemed one car in particular was following every turn I took. And I wasn't sure if my gasoline was going to hold out. I was an emotional wreck, praying to the Lord to help me get back to civilization and to the safety of people and light. When I finally emerged onto a road that my GPS recognized and that could get me to the venue, I felt giddy with the realization that I was going to make it. I didn't have the emotional resources to laugh aloud just then, but my insides were cracking jokes and giving high fives!

The woman in Jesus' parable must have felt something similar. While she sweeps and looks, she is anxious with that awful, gut-churning dread of losing something irreplaceable. But when she finds it, she has to throw a get-together. She calls her friends and neighbors and invites them to rejoice with her. And I don't know of a better way to do that than to laugh!

Have you lost something? Have you unexpectedly found it again?

Take a cue from this woman and rejoice. Give a good belly laugh and make the moment last. We have too many "lost" moments; let's lean into the "found" ones.

God, thank You for finding me when I was lost. Thank You for the unexpected delight when I find something I have lost. Remind me that Your heart beats for lost people, and help me to do all I can to bring them into reconciliation with You. In Jesus' name, amen.

Laughing in the Human Moments

Then our mouth was filled with laughter,
and our tongue with shouts of joy.
PSALM 126:2 ESV

I don't like to laugh at myself. It's one of my worst flaws. I love the strong sense of self people possess who can do it, but it's something I'm still working on.

Perhaps it's hard to laugh at ourselves because it makes us feel foolish for doing something laughable. Goofs always seem to look worse on us than on others.

We often comment on our "humanness." It certainly is a reason for our errors in judgment, social skills, and sometimes just blind spots. But it is also the lovable part of us.

When we unexpectedly commit a faux pas, we indicate that we are part of the human race, not something extraordinary, not someone above everyone else, but just normal like the rest of the folks around us. There is something warming about that.

Personally, I think Jesus had a sense of humor and liked to laugh. Now, He never sinned in any way and He had perfect judgment, but I wonder if He laughed at the little things that happened around Him. I think He and His disciples had relaxing, enjoyable moments as they traveled and camped together and ministered together. When a group of people live in close proximity for any length of time, funny things happen. And there is opportunity for pranks and banter. I don't know that Jesus ever had a need to laugh at Himself, but He certainly identified with the humanity in us that needs light moments from time to time.

Some of my most embarrassing moments have been the result of my words coming out wrong or an error in spatial judgment causing me to bump into something or fall. At such times, others find their mouths filled with laughter as the verse says, but I am more likely to feel my face burning with humiliation.

The delicate balance is learning to laugh at our humanness and yet not guffaw the loudest at the gaffe of a friend. Today you may have the opportunity to practice this. Do it well.

Lord, thank You for laughter and for the common human bond
I share with those around me. Help me to be mature enough
to smile at my own goofs and yet give grace to
those of people in my life. Amen.

Laughing at Impossibilities

*And Sarah said, "God has made laughter for me; everyone who
hears will laugh over me." And she said, "Who would have
said to Abraham that Sarah would nurse children?
Yet I have borne him a son in his old age."*
GENESIS 21:6–7 ESV

Sarah was old and her womb was withered. Dead. That's what the Bible says (Romans 4:19). She didn't expect to birth a child. And she certainly didn't expect to laugh. But she did both. In God's time.

The name Isaac means "laughter." And he certainly brought that to a hundred-year-old man and his ninety-year-old bride when he arrived. Those two elderly people laughed like they never had before as they watched a tiny baby boy wriggle and learn to crawl and give big grins and run around all over their nomadic camp. It was the fulfillment of God's promise. And Sarah knew her story would amuse people for all time. She knew we'd smile at the thought of her joy at finally receiving motherhood when she should have been sitting around in retirement.

I've always been interested in the fact that Sarah seemed to laugh in disbelief in the account told in Genesis 18 when the preincarnate Christ visited the tents of Abram and promised him a son. If I were God, I think I would have been indignant at the idea that a mere human would laugh at the promise. But God isn't like me. He is so far above us that He can see all the things we can't. He surely understood that to Sarah it was like a joke. And because they didn't have His Word to read like we do, which tells of all the impossibilities He can accomplish, and because He hadn't spoken to her before of it, He could see the heartbreak behind the laugh and the desperate hope that it might be true.

What are you hoping for that seems impossible? Can you believe that God might bring it to pass? Can you imagine that someday you might be laughing in delight at the fulfillment of a promise? It might seem just as impossible as a postmenopausal woman giving birth, but God can do the impossible. "Is anything too hard for the LORD?" (Genesis 18:14 ESV).

Pray for God's will. Believe in His plan. And you might be laughing sooner than you think.

Jehovah God, You are the One who can bring laughter into my life.
I ask You to be at work in all the impossibilities about which
I am praying. I trust that You can do anything. Amen.

Laughing in Victory

*When the LORD brought back the captivity of Zion, we were
like those who dream. Then our mouth was filled with laughter,
and our tongue with singing. Then they said among the
nations, "The LORD has done great things for them."
The LORD has done great things for us, and we are glad.*
PSALM 126:1–3 NKJV

There is no better laughter than what bubbles up inside us when a victory is won or a captive is set free.

One of the most tragic news items in our world is the recurring headlines about missing children. The horror endured by the parents is impossible to imagine. A parent's heart wants to protect and nurture the innocent little ones in their care, and the idea of the torture they might be experiencing is agonizing.

Many times the tales end in terrible sadness—a body found, a perpetrator caught, a story revealed. And sometimes there is no ending, only the ongoing anguish of wondering.

But every once in a while, there is a happy ending, a reunion. The child is returned to her parents. And there are smiles and joy, and laughter isn't far behind.

Sometimes there is laughter when a spiritual captive is returned. If you've ever witnessed the scene of a parent and child embracing after a prayer to come to Christ, you may have seen it for yourself. There are tight hugs and backslaps and smiles, and sometimes laughter. The delight inside bubbles up and spills over.

These things happen unexpectedly for us because we can't see what is going on in the spiritual world. God knows the end from the beginning and oversees the progression of events. But for us, all of a sudden, one day the captive is freed and the spiritual victory is won.

Someday God will set this world free from the curse of sin, and Satan will be cast into eternal fire. The victory of God's kingdom will be complete, and we will reign with Christ forever. Only the Father knows when that day is coming, but we are secure in the knowledge that it is a specific date on His timetable. And when that unexpected and glorious day arrives, we will have joy like we've never had it before.

*Heavenly Father, You rejoice every time a spiritual captive is
set free by Your power. You hold all future events in Your hands.
Today I want to live with the anticipation of Your final victory. Amen.*

Laughing at the Feast

A feast is made for laughter.
ECCLESIASTES 10:19 KJV

There are some places where you expect to laugh, right? A comedy show. A concert. A party. A reunion.

The wisdom writer said that feasts are exactly the right place for laughter. One is made for the other.

Ancient custom forbade a long face in the presence of the king. In fact, it might even be reason for an instant execution! One was supposed to show positivity of spirit and joy of countenance when approaching the throne. Some kings even employed their own entertainer, the court jester, to tell jokes or perform antics and keep the atmosphere jolly.

Remember the story of Esther? She was nervous about walking into the king's presence without an invitation. That was also forbidden on threat of death. Such was the strict regulation that controlled the palace in biblical times.

Our God sits on the throne of heaven. He reigns over our world and the galaxies beyond. Yet He allows us to approach Him with our raw emotions and with downcast faces.

Hebrews 4:16 says that we may approach God's throne boldly and find grace to help us in our time of need. Our God doesn't demand that we make Him feel good; He reaches out to us to bring us good.

Someday every believing child of God will be gathered in one place for the greatest feast of all. It's called the marriage supper of the Lamb (Revelation 19:9). There the King will celebrate the marriage of His Son, Jesus, to His bride, the church. And there will be great joy and laughter like we've never known. Laughter that lasts for eternity.

Who would ever have imagined that the God who made everything would throw a great feast and invite us to it? That's an unexpected welcome. But He did. And He doesn't want anyone to miss it.

Father, I'm so glad You made room for all of us at Your great feast. Thank You for including me. Because I have put my faith in Christ, I am looking forward to the joy and laughter of that day. Amen.

UNEXPECTED LOVE

Unknown Wonder

Then the rib which the LORD God had taken from man He
made into a woman, and He brought her to the man.
GENESIS 2:22 NKJV

The best kind of love stories are the unexpected ones, the kind where two people meet by "chance" or where an ordinary happening results in extraordinary romance. We women never tire of this kind of story line. Perhaps it's because of the plot of the first romance on earth.

Her name was Eve. Her husband named her. And he had never seen a woman before. He didn't even know such creatures existed. Actually, she didn't until God made her out of his bone.

When he woke up from his nap (during which God performed surgery), Adam looked around and saw that the Creator had left him a surprise—her.

Think of what this love story was like. They must have both spoken the same language, whatever it was. He reached out to her. What did he say? Did he touch her smooth skin with wonder? With his perfect brain and reasoning, he must have known that God had given him a mate, a companion wonderfully suited for him and gloriously different at the same time. The awe of that first meeting of male and female had to be something glorious. And God said it was very good.

Every feminine heart longs for that kind of wonder. We yearn to be gazed at with amazement. It's the reason women spend so much money on cosmetics and so many hours at the gym. We want to recapture the glory Eve had, the indefinable attraction that entranced Adam.

The serpent and his temptation spoiled forever the enchanting romance in the garden. And hard as we try to regain the spark, something was distorted then that still haunts our love stories. But we know, deep in our souls, that we were made for that kind of wonder, and we long for it still.

Someday we will be given to Christ as His bride. The magnificence of that moment will outshine any other. For the garden awe is only a tiny glimmer of the eternal splendor. And the Creator who ordained earthly romance has something far better to reveal in that day.

Father, my feminine heart was made to thrill with romance. And I am so glad that I am part of the bride of Christ through my faith in Your Son. Until that day, keep my affections focused on You. Thank You for Your unending love. Amen.

Precious Expressions

A word fitly spoken is like apples of gold in settings of silver.
PROVERBS 25:11 NKJV

Have you ever found a surprise note? A note from someone special to you?

I have. It makes your heart skip a beat or two when you find a note from your sweetheart stuck under your windshield wiper or in your purse or maybe under your pillow. I sometimes send notes in my husband's suitcase when he's away on trips. There's just something about a written expression of love that makes all of us happy.

I have also discovered notes from my children. When they were little and learning to write, they'd give me the sweetest little missives, with jerky letters and misspelled words, but precious beyond price to me. As they got older, they would sometimes leave little notes at special times. One from my daughter thanked me for cooking good meals. And a note when she was much older thanked me for working so our children could attend a Christian school. Another daughter left me a note when she went to college and knew I was having a difficult time adjusting to that change. My Bible still contains notes that they have written to me, reminders of love.

The writer of Proverbs describes how special these words are with terms of precious metals—gold and silver. Words gifted to us from dear ones are truly that meaningful.

Every note we've ever received is only the tiniest glimpse of the great heart of God toward us. David wrote about it in Psalm 139:17–18 (NKJV): "How precious also are Your thoughts to me, O God! How great is the sum of them! If I should count them, they would be more in number than the sand; when I awake, I am still with You."

You may not think of it this way, but every morning when you wake up, God is sending you a note. The sun shining outside your window, the oxygen circulating in your bedroom, the birds chirping on the branches, the people who populate your day—these are the expressions of love He puts in your life.

Sometimes God sends something out of the ordinary; sometimes it's just the blessedness of nontraumatic routine. Look for His message in your life today.

Father, Your heart of love toward me overwhelms me.
Thank You for showing Your love to me in so many ways.
I want to pass it on to others. In Jesus' name, amen.

The Solid Kind of Love

"But I say to you, love your enemies, bless those who curse you,
do good to those who hate you, and pray for those
who spitefully use you and persecute you."
MATTHEW 5:44 NKJV

Do you want to do something completely wild?

Love someone who doesn't like you.

That's right. The most unexpected, most Christlike gift you can give is to love those who mistreat you and hate you. No other amazement is quite like what your enemy will experience if you do.

We often think of unexpected blessings coming to us, but what if we are the source of unexpected blessing for someone else? That is when we are like our Father in heaven. He calls us to be like Him, and that includes patterning our interactions with others after the way He does things. The apostle Peter wrote that we can be "partakers of the divine nature" (2 Peter 1:4 ESV). What an astounding realization! Because of the Holy Spirit's work in us, we can imitate our Lord and actually have His nature inside us.

Sometimes at parties there is a white elephant gift exchange. This silly little game is simply the fun of exchanging corny, impractical gifts. One might be especially desirable, but generally none of them are worth much except for laughs. Part of the hilarity is tearing off the wrapping and discovering what ridiculous thing is inside.

But the kind of love we have to share with our enemies, while it might be surprising, is never frivolous nor silly. It is the most solid, genuine love there can be, because it comes from the heart of God through us.

Heavenly Father, give me the grace to love those who mistreat me. In Your strength, I make the choice to bless those who curse me and do good to those who hate me. I depend on Your love to flow through me. In Jesus' name, amen.

Finding the Backstage

*"For God commanded, 'Honor your father and your mother,'
and, 'Whoever reviles father or mother must surely die.' "*
MATTHEW 15:4 ESV

My mother used to tell me that I could show her I loved her by my obedience.

It's true, isn't it? Jesus said, "If you love me, you will keep my commandments" (John 14:15 ESV).

A child who is old enough to understand what rebellion is can understand that words of endearment mean nothing when the appropriate actions don't follow.

God said about His wayward children that they "draw near with their mouth and honor me with their lips, while their hearts are far from me" (Isaiah 29:13 ESV). The deep feelings of our hearts are always revealed in our actions.

And when parents begin to age and need extra care, children can show their love in how they respond to their needs. The tables are turned, and the once cared for become the caregivers. It happens when we're not looking. One day they're capable and healthy, involved in the full spectrum of life, and the next, they are fragile and a little unsteady, taking things slower and resting more often.

Our acceptance of the twists in life can turn into great blessings. When our parents can no longer teach us about doing things in life, they begin to teach us about accepting help in life. They model for us how to back off of center stage, how to find contentment in the shadows, how to make a front porch a sanctuary and a kitchen table an altar.

Aging is something that happens gradually. I remember discovering my first gray hair when I was in my thirties. But aging begins earlier than that. From the moment of birth, we begin to die. From the point of physical maturity, we begin to decline. And the sudden realization that there is more behind us than in front of us is startling. Our parents will reach that before we do. And then we can continue the honor we began when they were strong and we were weak. We can love them not only with words but with service.

Heavenly Father, You are the God of every season and every generation. You will care for us always. Help me to be Your love in action to my parents in every stage of life. Amen.

Spontaneous Actions

So she quickly emptied her jar into the trough and ran again
to the well to draw water, and she drew for all his camels.
The man gazed at her in silence to learn whether
the LORD had prospered his journey or not.
GENESIS 24:20–21 ESV

It's highly unlikely to receive a marriage proposal while you're watering animals. But that's what happened to Rebekah.

It was chore time. She was doing what women in the household did—going to the well for water. And her spontaneous act of kindness toward the stranger with the caravan of camels was the thing that secured her future.

Abraham had commissioned his trusted servant to find a wife for his son. He didn't want Isaac to marry a pagan woman from the Canaanites. And so the servant had a plan. And Rebekah did exactly as he had asked the Lord for her to do in order to give him a sign that she was the right woman for his master. And the rest, as they say, is history. After talking with her family and doing some deep thinking, she decided to return with the servant and marry a man she had never seen, the child of promise grown up, the beginning of the great Hebrew nation.

What were you doing when you met the man you would marry? Something menial? Something unusual? Did it have anything to do with the life you now share together?

I wonder if we would be more attuned to the significance of everyday actions if we remembered that someone might be watching how we perform them for a specific reason. Perhaps our responses and offers of help guide others in knowing how God is leading them. Maybe they are watching us in silence like the servant did to see if God is showing up in this ordinary place.

They made the long journey back across the desert, and Rebekah's first glimpse of Isaac was of him walking in the field, meditating. She asked who he was and then veiled herself as propriety demanded in those days. Only a husband could view a woman unveiled. And Isaac took her as his wife and loved her. Her love brought him comfort after the death of his mother, Sarah.

Rebekah couldn't have dreamed when she went to the well that day that her life was going to change so drastically. You might not know how the events that are happening right now are changing your future. But God does. And He guides caravans and chore time and every other detail if we let Him.

God, You are the One who sees every tiny detail of my life. I'm not sure how my tomorrows connect with my activities today, but I trust You to work all things out in Your time. For Jesus' sake, amen.

UNEXPECTED TRIALS

Refining Tools

*"For affliction does not come from the dust,
nor does trouble sprout from the ground, but man
is born to trouble as the sparks fly upward."*
JOB 5:6–7 ESV

Some days Job's statement in Job 5:6–7 could be a life verse. Trouble—difficulties and challenges large and small—comes at us in a variety of ways.

The dishwasher stops working. Mine did. It hadn't been cleaning dishes right for a while, but I babied it along, rinsing the dishes after they came out and trying to make sure I kept the apparatus working. Then the computerized system went haywire and it started turning itself on. That was a problem. Finally, it just was unusable.

Another day, I put the wet laundry into the dryer and selected the setting I wanted. An hour later when I pulled them out, they were cool and very damp. The heating element had gone bad.

The bathtub drain clogged. The battery in the garage door opener died. The Keurig sputtered and spit at me. The minivan decided not to run. All of these little inconveniences mark the truth of Job's exasperated proclamation—man is born to trouble.

These kinds of minor calamities come upon us randomly and without warning. That's the way life changes. There is no announcement, no "Get ready for trouble!" No, it just arrives like an undesired guest.

Today you may be facing some small troubles that seem big at the moment. Remember that God is in the little things too, and He is using every unplanned moment to shape you even closer to His image. And if Job can survive his disasters, so can you. The God he worshipped is there for you when you call.

Dear Lord, take my unwanted moments and make them into refining tools to shape me closer to Your image. Thank You for being there in my dark times. Amen.

Really Bad Days

"For we have been sold, I and my people, to be destroyed, to be killed, and to be annihilated."

ESTHER 7:4 ESV

We've all had bad days. But probably none of us have found out that our entire race of people was destined for extinction. That was what Esther was told. As the new queen, she had busy days and nights and little time for frivolous concerns. But when her cousin Mordecai informed her of the plot against the Jewish nation, she listened. He beseeched her to help from her position of power. She knew that she might die before she had the chance to tell the king the problem. But she would die anyway from the edict, so she decided to take the risk.

Esther hadn't lived a charmed life. Her parents were killed when she was young, and she was a member of an oppressed people living captive in a foreign land. She was raised by her cousin and protected by him up until the day the king commanded that every eligible young virgin in the city be rounded up as potential queen material. When we read the story now, we think of the glamour of the Persian palace and the fascination of the beauty routines. But for Esther it was a still more intense form of captivity. She would never be able to leave the harem once she spent the night with the king. She would be part of a petted, protected gaggle of women who lived out their lives in luxury and loneliness.

When she unexpectedly became the queen, Esther was no doubt happy that her life would have purpose. But then the words of Mordecai made her realize that she was still vulnerable to trouble.

Maybe, like Esther, you have had a difficult life, and just when things seemed about to open up for you, a bigger problem than ever dropped into your path. Take courage from the resolve of a young queen trying to save her people.

"Go, gather all the Jews to be found in Susa, and hold a fast on my behalf, and do not eat or drink for three days, night or day. I and my young women will also fast as you do. Then I will go to the king, though it is against the law, and if I perish, I perish" (Esther 4:16 ESV).

Don't be alarmed at the trouble; be resolute in your heart. Bad days are meant to be conquered, and we know the God who can do anything.

Father in heaven, like Esther, I trust You today to give me a plan to deal with my trouble. This challenge of mine did not surprise You, and I need Your help as I deal with it. Thank You for Your constant care. Amen.

UNEXPECTED POWER

Grace for Our Groans

*And He said to me, "My grace is sufficient for you, for My strength
is made perfect in weakness." Therefore most gladly I will rather
boast in my infirmities, that the power of Christ may rest upon
me. Therefore I take pleasure in infirmities, in reproaches,
in needs, in persecutions, in distresses, for Christ's sake.
For when I am weak, then I am strong.*
2 Corinthians 12:9–10 NKJV

Disabilities and afflictions are not usually the image in our minds when
we think of power. Rather, they depict weakness. But the apostle Paul,
under the inspiration of the Holy Spirit, said that's okay. When we're at
our weakest, Christ is showing His strength.

I don't enjoy doctor's office waiting rooms. They're holding tanks for
people with miseries. I know. I've been one of them. The cushy chairs
and modern art and cheerful fish aquarium can't completely block the
thoughts from your mind that there is something wrong with you and
you need help. The folks around you are in various states of suffering,
depending on which kind of specialist you're seeing. Usually, you can see
evidence of their maladies on them or beside them—bandages, casts,
canes, patches, oxygen tanks, and the like. And when the next name
is called at the door, someone lumbers to his or her feet and shuffles
off, hoping for a new miracle drug. Sounds pretty depressing. And of
course, physical ailments aren't the only kind with which we contend.
Mental and emotional distress can be "thorns in our flesh" as well.

No one knows for sure what indisposition Paul had, though there have been many guesses. Some say it was his eyesight; others say something else. No matter, because the principle applies to us all in whatever we face.

You can find astounding, unexpected power in your weakest moment. It won't be the kind that lifts you off your bed and makes you want to run a marathon. It won't be the type that makes you feel completely happy in the middle of your battle with the blues. But it will be a power that gives you strength to accept the challenge of the next hour. It will be the grace that helps you make a decision, face the day, receive encouragement from friends.

I don't know what weakness is in your path today—chemotherapy, surgery, bed rest, diagnostic tests, dialysis, physical therapy, organ transplant—but the God of strength does. And He can give the power.

Father, I need power for my weakness today.
I trust You for it. Amen.

His Name in the Night

I remember Your name in the night, O Lord.
Psalm 119:55 NKJV

Night brings many terrors and anxieties. Trees stand taller. Buildings loom larger. Corners descend deeper. Noises echo louder. Fears clutch tighter. Regrets swirl faster. Dread churns harder.

Night is a time when we feel less capable. The absence of light and the coming alive of the nocturnal world give familiar things and places an eeriness that we know we shouldn't care about but do anyway.

In the night, we need power. Power to rest, power to rejuvenate, power to relinquish all things into the Almighty's hands.

Psalm 119 is a passage in which every verse contains some reference to the Word of God. Different names are used, but each of them pertains in some way to the wonderful treasure we have in scripture. In verse 55, the writer recommends an action we can use to fight our overwhelming weakness as the daylight fades and dusk approaches.

We can remember His name:

Jehovah—Provider
Lord—Sovereign
Messiah—Promised One
Jesus—Savior
Almighty God
Everlasting Father
Prince of peace
King of kings
Friend

In every unexpected nighttime moment, His name has the comfort we seek. And His power is revealed if we choose to believe in Him. There is no need to toss and turn alone in the night. Grab hold of His name and believe who He is.

Lord Jesus, You are life and peace and all I need tonight.
I trust the power in Your name for the unrest in my heart. Amen.

Escape from the Prowler

No temptation has overtaken you except such as is common to man; but God is faithful, who will not allow you to be tempted beyond what you are able, but with the temptation will also make the way of escape, that you may be able to bear it.

1 CORINTHIANS 10:13 NKJV

Temptation is like a bacteria lurking, a predator stalking, a beast prowling. It is always swirling in the air, always tracking our location, always watching for an opportunity. The words Paul was inspired to write in 1 Corinthians 10:13 seem to indicate that a specific temptation dogs our steps until it catches up to us. We cannot escape the reality of temptation in this life. Even Jesus, the perfect Son of God, was tempted to sin. But He didn't yield. And because He conquered temptation, so can we. "For in that He Himself has suffered, being tempted, He is able to aid those who are tempted" (Hebrews 2:18 NKJV).

Temptation appeals to our weakness. It comes to us when our power is low, when we are tired or hungry or stressed or even relaxed and our guard is down. It comes to us in a moment when the evil offer makes sense in light of our needs. Remember Jesus' temptation by Satan in the wilderness. He was alone and hungry and physically weak, and Satan saw an opportunity. "And when He had fasted forty days and forty nights, afterward He was hungry. Now when the tempter came to Him, he said, 'If You are the Son of God, command that these stones become bread' " (Matthew 4:2–3 NKJV).

Satan does the same to us. He zeroes in on our natural frailties or the strategic vulnerability of an unguarded moment of extremity and makes his play.

But the power of Christ is ours through the Holy Spirit. Jesus used the Word of God to resist. The truth wielded against the enemy will always win. We must put His truth on constant patrol in our hearts and minds so that the blitz of the enemy can be thwarted.

We are promised a way of escape. We are promised His presence. We are promised power.

Father God, I want Your power of Christ when I face temptation. Give me determination to focus on Your Word, and open my eyes to the way of escape You provide. In the name of Jesus, amen.

A Mother's Miracle

So she went from him and shut the door behind herself and
her sons. And as she poured they brought the vessels to her.
When the vessels were full, she said to her son, "Bring me
another vessel." And he said to her, "There is not
another." Then the oil stopped flowing.

2 KINGS 4:5–6 ESV

Times are tough for single moms today, but I think they're a little better than they were in ancient times. Take this woman's story.

Her husband, a prophet, died. And the family had some debts that were due. Children were one of a family's most valuable assets, and a creditor could put them into indentured service to pay off the money owed. This woman knew this was going to happen, so she went to the man of God for advice.

Do you remember the story? He asked what she had of value in her home, and all she had was a jar of oil. But it was a valuable commodity that could be sold. There just wasn't much of it. Now here's where the miracle began. Acting on his advice, she borrowed containers from everyone she knew and then filled them from her jar. Wait a minute! Yes, that's right. The jar became a warehouse supply of oil. She could sell the oil in the containers to pay the debt. (Maybe she also paid her neighbors for the containers—I've always wondered about that!) At any rate, her sons were spared, and her debts were paid. Talk about relief and gratefulness!

God cares about your mothering situation today. He sees the miracle you need. The Bible tells us that He is especially near to the widow and the fatherless. "Father of the fatherless and protector of widows is God in his holy habitation" (Psalm 68:5 ESV).

There is no situation that faces you or your children where He is not sovereign. When friends can't help, He can. When social programs fall short, He is there. When you are alone, He is nearby.

I have a friend who has found herself tragically alone as a single mom. The care of her three small children has fallen solidly on her shoulders. She has had to grieve the heartache of her aloneness as well as try to be mother and father to little ones who don't understand all the reasons. She has suffered much. At times I wonder how a person can endure such heartrending circumstances. But I know she has seen the truth of Psalm 68:5. God has been their support and tower, and He has used His people to show that in a tangible way.

You may feel alone with your mom needs, but you aren't. Take them to the One who uses jars of oil to pay debts. He'll make a way for you.

Father in heaven, I bring You my need today. You see my children and their vulnerability. You understand my helplessness right now. Please do the work that only You can do. Amen.

Debtors Who Forgive

*Be kind to one another, tenderhearted,
forgiving one another, even as God in Christ forgave you.*
EPHESIANS 4:32 NKJV

Forgiveness is a theme about which there are varying opinions. Many of them are based on the ideas that make sense to us as humans. But they are all flawed in some way. That's because forgiveness is a divine concept and must be understood through the words of the One who instituted it.

Prevalent ideas about forgiveness focus on feeling charitable toward the perpetrator of the wrong. The belief is that I must feel forgiving in order to be forgiving. This is not so. Forgiveness is an act of the will; it is based on my decision to seek the other's good instead of harm.

Forgiveness is our responsibility as receivers of God's forgiveness to us. We cannot hoard for ourselves this mercy we've been given and then turn on others with retribution. No, we are debtors to grace to pass on the gift of forgiveness.

The power of forgiveness comes when we need it, when we make the choice to obey God's command to forgive. I do not need the grace to forgive unless I have been sinned against. In the moment when my realization of the wrong done collides with my awareness that I cannot hold this memory in my heart, I can turn to Christ and expect that He will help me. He has promised to do so.

Dear Father, thank You for forgiving me. I know that Your power will be there in those moments when I need to forgive others. I rest in this today. Amen.

Sudden Healing

Now a woman, having a flow of blood for twelve years, who had spent all her livelihood on physicians and could not be healed by any, came from behind and touched the border of His garment. And immediately her flow of blood stopped.

LUKE 8:43–44 NKJV

Having a menstrual disorder is inconvenient and life altering in any culture, but for a Jewish woman, few things were worse. Because of the ceremonial purity laws, a woman with an ongoing menstrual flow was unclean and could not mingle in public, attend religious ceremonies, or even be close to her family. They would all be considered unclean from touching her or anything she touched. She was, for all intents and purposes, isolated.

Behind the purity laws, of course, was a good God who cared about His people. For the protection of women during their bodily processes and for the control of disease in a culture that didn't understand bacteria and sanitation, He had instituted strict laws to govern His people's lifestyles. This was to keep them from having many of the problems other nations had. But in cases like hers, the laws prevented her from living a normal life.

She'd heard about Jesus. And she believed He might be her answer, her healing.

Think about what it took for her to get to Him. She was probably weak. Blood loss for twelve years depletes the body and leads to anemia and extreme fatigue during any kind of exertion. Maybe she was actually on her hands and knees from weakness and that was how she happened to be near the hem of His garment. We don't know. But we do know she had faith. Jesus proclaimed that her faith had made her whole.

Immediately, the blood loss stopped. She was healed instantly. Something she had longed for and had spent all her money on did happen in a moment.

What condition have you fought for years? What spiritual anemia has made you weak? Come to Jesus in faith. We cannot see Him with our physical eyes, but we can see Him with the eyes of faith.

"Blessed are those who have not seen and yet have believed" (John 20:29 NKJV).

Dear Lord, thank You for the healing You bring to bodies and to souls. Today I reach out by faith and believe You can heal the spiritual need I have. Amen.

The Practice of Silence

To everything there is a season, a time for every purpose under heaven. . .a time to keep silence, and a time to speak.
ECCLESIASTES 3:1, 7 NKJV

Realizing that there is a time for silence is not welcome. Once we learn to express ourselves in words, we like to give opinions, not listen to them. But God's Word tells us that silence helps us grow and learn. And there are times when we must practice it.

Silence makes me think of two religious practices in particular. One is the vow of silence practiced by some monastic orders as a tool in drawing near to God. Those who undertake this vow have varying guidelines to follow, but all involve some restriction on the spoken word for a specified period of time.

The other example is that of the Quakers, or Society of Friends, whose tradition it was—and still is in some places—to sit in silence in the meetinghouse and wait for the Spirit to move upon a brother or sister with a word from God for all.

Both of these illustrations, whether we agree with them or not, indicate that silence can be a means of quieting ourselves and listening for the voice of God. Oftentimes the clamor of my own thoughts is as loud as the other noise in my setting. It follows, then, that silence must be learned in the heart as well as by the mouth.

Psalm 46:10 (NKJV) admonishes us to "be still, and know" in our hearts that the Lord is God. The silence we need to embrace must fill our beings and usher our souls into His presence so we can hear His voice.

The power of silence in difficult moments is especially challenging, but the Holy Spirit is faithful to check us in those moments so that we can turn to Him for strength. Silence can be healing, restorative, merciful, and loving. This is the power that He wants to show through us.

Dear Lord, I need to learn the grace of silence. I ask You to give me the power to hold my tongue at the appropriate times as I listen to Your Spirit's caution. In Jesus' name, amen.

"For thus says the LORD, the God of Israel, 'The jar of flour shall not be spent, and the jug of oil shall not be empty, until the day that the LORD sends rain upon the earth.' " And she went and did as Elijah said. And she and he and her household ate for many days. The jar of flour was not spent, neither did the jug of oil become empty, according to the word of the LORD that he spoke by Elijah.

1 KINGS 17:14–16 ESV

The closest I have come to experiencing a famine was in the aftermath of a hurricane in central Florida. The storm season was severe that year, and several of them made landfall and traveled inland. Our family rode out this particular one, though we lost our electricity and had to rough it for a few days. But overall we fared very well. Damage was all around us but nothing catastrophic.

I graphically remember going to the local grocery store and finding a very different scene from the norm. The lights were out, and the emergency lighting made the atmosphere very dim. All the meats and delicate refrigerated and frozen items had gone bad from the lack of electricity, and black plastic covered the freezers and cold bins. The shelves containing bread and peanut butter and crackers were bare. It was a startling sight and a reminder of how fragile is our way of life. A storm of nature can destroy the balance of the technological advances on which we depend.

The prophet Elijah was in the middle of a famine. God had withheld rain at his request and had taken care of him through supernatural means. But now he was told to find a widow in Zarephath and stay at her home for a time. Surely God's intention was also to bring hope and rescue to this woman as well, since God could have taken care of the prophet any other way He chose.

When Elijah found her and heard her pitiful story, he gave her instructions. And because she was willing to obey, they survived the famine and drought. Her story has been told and retold as an example of God's provision when we obey what we know to do.

You probably need the power of provision in some area of your life today. I encourage you to reach out to the One who puts us in certain places so that His power can be revealed. Don't despair. You may be gathering sticks for your last fire, but God is already planning the miracle you need.

Father God, You are the source of all provision. You oversee all the conditions that affect the story we have today. I ask You to work in my famine today for Your glory. In Jesus' name, amen.

Mothers and Flocks

He will feed His flock like a shepherd; He will gather the
lambs with His arm, and carry them in His bosom,
and gently lead those who are with young.
Isaiah 40:11 NKJV

Motherhood is an enormous job, a staggering proposition. You take on the total welfare of another human. And you are intricately emotionally connected to him or her for life.

Mothering has been compared to many things. And every year, the greeting card companies try to come up with new ways to applaud the endless contributions of mothers. Maybe you've never seen a card comparing a human mom to a sheep, but both are intense mothers.

Ewe sheep are protective and nurturing and like their lambs within sight. They even use a special language only with their children.

Human mothers also feel a deep bond with their children, even after they've grown. Yet despite the fact that they are lauded and affirmed, mothers struggle with unbelievable amounts of guilt. Images to which we may compare ourselves abound, and there is no shortage of material to tell us how to do things better. It's no wonder that some feel more guilt than joy on Mother's Day.

God understands moms. He made them. He thought up the whole idea in the first place. And He has promised to help moms with their task.

The prophet Isaiah, writing to Israel, God's beloved, communicated Jehovah's love for them and His commitment to their future welfare, especially the longevity of Jerusalem, often called the Daughter of Zion. Isaiah pictured the Lord as a Shepherd who comes to lead His people and will gently lead those who have young.

While this passage may first have a spiritual application, we can also see its relevance for moms. Our Lord does not drive us; He gently leads us when we need it. He understands the demands of mothering. We can trust His skill and compassion, His tender care of us and our little ones.

Gentle Shepherd, thank You for leading me and all the mothers with young. May we look to You for power in the moments when mothering overwhelms us. And may we belong to Your great flock for eternity. In Jesus' name, amen.

Power of a Voice

She, supposing Him to be the gardener, said to Him, "Sir, if You have carried Him away, tell me where You have laid Him, and I will take Him away." Jesus said to her, "Mary!" She turned and said to Him, "Rabboni!" (which is to say, Teacher).
JOHN 20:15–16 NKJV

Mary couldn't stop crying. The weekend had been the worst of her life. The Rabbi, the Lord, who had cast demons from her and changed her life from misery to joy, had been crucified like a criminal. Earthquakes had wracked the city. The believers were in hiding, afraid of reprisals. And now when Mary and her friends had come to anoint His body, they'd discovered that it apparently had been taken to another location.

She was crushed. She could not fulfill a last service to the One who had given her back her life. The two men in white in the tomb asked her why she was weeping, and she tried to explain. Then she turned and saw Jesus, but she didn't know it was Him. Through her tears, He looked like one of the workmen there. She asked, "Where have you taken my Lord?"

And then He spoke her name: "Mary." And she knew that voice. It was the voice that had called to her when her mind was imprisoned in hell on earth. It was the voice she had heard from a distance as the darkness left her soul and light came flooding in. It was His voice, the voice of life.

Mary Magdalene had twice received unexpected joy. The first was when Jesus cast seven spirits from her (see Luke 8:2), and the second was when He cast away her despair on Easter morning.

Perhaps you too need to hear the power of Jesus' voice. Today voices everywhere are creating fear and anxiety and dread. But His voice brings freedom and joy.

Heavenly Father, thank You for sending Your Son to speak peace to our world. Thank You for the power of His voice and the power of His resurrection that triumphs over everything. Like Mary, I worship You today. Amen.

Braking Power

*Train the young women to love their husbands and children, to be
self-controlled, pure, working at home, kind, and submissive to
their own husbands, that the word of God may not be reviled.*

TITUS 2:4–5 ESV

I enjoy takeoff more than landing. The exhilaration of the thrust of the
engines and that catch of the wings into the current is incredible time
after time.

Landing, on the other hand, always makes me just a little anxious.
Will those brakes hold? Why does it feel like we are squealing down
the last few feet of runway and about to run out of room?

It's so much easier to power up than pull back. And to me, this can
illustrate submission.

God put the structure of submission into our world. It holds together
the mechanics we need for the family, the church, and society in general.
An authority structure is necessary for work to be done and progress
to be made.

Ephesians 5:21 says that we are to submit to one another in the
fear of God. This is a general scriptural principle that all of us must
follow. We must submit to the plan He ordered. And it is specifically
delineated in 1 Corinthians 11:3 (ESV): "I want you to understand that
the head of every man is Christ, the head of a wife is her husband, and
the head of Christ is God." This is God's pattern for getting things done
in our world and for the beautiful harmony in our relationships. Selfish
application will always result in tragedy, but honest, loving conformity
allows healthy relationships.

None of us, man or woman, enjoys the submitting part. We would rather do the takeoff. But the pulling back, the putting on of brakes, the acknowledging of proper order must happen if the flight can be successful.

Culture will tell you to take orders from no one, to stand up for your way. God tells us that submitting to the head over us keeps our rebellious tendencies from ruling us and brings us into the mind of Christ who submitted to the Father's will and took on the "form of a servant" (Philippians 2:7 KJV). This is the crucial power—applying the brakes at the right time.

Dear God, You have ordained a beautiful structure in our world. I want to honor it in my life. I ask for Your power so I may fit into my place. In Jesus' name, amen.

The Warmth of Welcome

Show hospitality to one another without grumbling.
1 PETER 4:9 ESV

Much of the allure of the fictional town of Mayberry, North Carolina, was in its hometown amenities. Friendly neighbors, front porches, a benevolent barber, and chatty gas station attendant all contributed to the charm of this little place that felt like home. Oh, and the hospitality. It was one of those places where you'd be offered a glass of iced tea or a cup of coffee and the chance to sit a spell.

Hospitality of that kind may be a lost art, or at least a disappearing art. First of all, most of us don't have time to make visits to our friends. And second, we'd be too worried about the house to invite them in if they came to ours.

Now, I'm not sure of the specifics of what Peter wrote in his first epistle to the churches, but I'm positive that warmth and welcome are implied. Christians are supposed to have open doors as well as open hearts. Of course this doesn't mean that we have no limits. If anything goes, soon nothing will be left! But it does mean that we share what we can as often as we can.

In the early church, Christians, of necessity, shared what they had with one another. The ostracism they felt from society and the marketplace, as well as the limited resources they had as outcasts, combined to raise significant challenges in eking out a living. Sharing with those who had need not only made sense but was a fulfillment of Jesus' command to love one another.

It's not quite the same in our day, but showing welcome to others is still a sign of a loving heart. If you're like me, though, you need extra energy to do it. Finding time to engage in social activities and even opening up your home for it adds more stress to the week, and most of us have full calendars already.

We do know that God gives us the power to complete the tasks He asks us to do. If hospitality is a trait of following Christ, then He will help us do it. We have to use common sense about family needs and our financial abilities. We have to be sure that we are doing so under the proper channels of church ministry. But we can take a risk and try something new.

Dear Lord, I want to give others the welcome that You have given me as Your child. Empower me to show hospitality in practical ways whenever I can, because it is a way to show my love for You. In Jesus' name, amen.

Mentoring Power

*Older women likewise are to be reverent in behavior,
not slanderers or slaves to much wine. They are to teach
what is good, and so train the young women.*

Titus 2:3–4 esv

Coffee chats. They're a social media thing. But they're also a Bible thing.

You've heard of mentoring, right? It's when a more mature Christ follower takes a less mature Christ follower under her wing by meeting regularly to talk about life and how the Bible applies to it. Mentoring is a life-enriching resource that is gaining momentum in our culture.

I don't know if they had the same kind of system in the New Testament days, but the idea that Titus is going for here applies. We are to teach others so they can in turn pass what they learn on to someone else. That's the heart of mentoring. And we need the Spirit's power to do it.

Younger women want to be mentored in the faith. Older women wish they could help the younger women. But both are afraid to make the first move. We need to break through our barriers and inhibitions and make it happen.

Mentoring works best when there is trust. Mentees and mentors must feel safe and have confidence that what is shared is privileged information. And because trust takes time, mentoring relationships progress slowly and become richer the longer we are in them.

Our local coffee shop is often the scene of meetings for conversation about the Bible. My husband and I see them—a couple of women or a meeting of two guys—with Bibles and notebooks open and a serious conversation taking place. It makes us happy every time we see it. It means that God's people are taking His Word seriously and that the

Christian community wants to continue to be shaped in biblical ways.

Maybe you need this means of grace in your life. Maybe you need to give instruction to someone else. Why not open your heart and ask the Lord for direction and power to accomplish it?

———∽◦

Dear Father, You have given others wisdom that I need. And I have wisdom to share with others. Empower me to find the channels through which I can share Your wisdom with others. In Christ's name, amen.

Power of Life

Now when the Sabbath was past, Mary Magdalene, Mary the mother of James, and Salome bought spices, that they might come and anoint Him. Very early in the morning, on the first day of the week, they came to the tomb when the sun had risen. And they said among themselves, "Who will roll away the stone from the door of the tomb for us?" But when they looked up, they saw that the stone had been rolled away—for it was very large. And entering the tomb, they saw a young man clothed in a long white robe sitting on the right side; and they were alarmed. But he said to them, "Do not be alarmed. You seek Jesus of Nazareth, who was crucified. He is risen! He is not here. See the place where they laid Him. But go, tell His disciples—and Peter—that He is going before you into Galilee; there you will see Him, as He said to you."

MARK 16:1–7 NKJV

Few things are more startling than an open grave, especially when you expect it to be closed. The women had been wondering who would roll away the massive stone, but they didn't expect it to be done for them already. They didn't realize it, but the power of the Almighty had moved that stone.

It was early morning and misty, and they were confused. No one had risen from the dead before. They hadn't been able to comprehend that Jesus meant that He would actually come out of the tomb after three days. They went inside to see if perhaps the body would still be there. It wasn't, but a young man in a white robe was. And he had an amazing message.

We've heard the Easter story so often that we miss the awe in the details. These were women just like you and me, going to perform a last burial rite for a beloved Friend. They knew the disciples were in hiding and that their future looked bleak. They knew that the Rabbi they'd all followed was dead. But somebody still had to take care of the things of life, and preparing the body was one of them. These women, like so many of us after a tragedy occurs, pushed back their tears and carried on with the mundane tasks of life. But today would be anything but mundane. Can you imagine what they thought when they heard the angel's words?

The news that Jesus had risen was just the beginning of a new chapter in the women's lives. Very soon they would be gathered with the other believers in a room above the city, waiting for the promise of His life in them through the power of the Holy Spirit. Very soon the world would know that things would never be the same. Very soon these women would be part of a movement that would march from Jerusalem into Judea and Samaria and the uttermost parts of the earth to proclaim the most unexpected message the world has ever heard—Jesus is risen and coming again!

Dear Father in heaven, thank You for raising Jesus from the dead and for giving His resurrection life to me through the power of the Holy Spirit. Please make my life a testament to the change He brings. In Jesus' name, amen.

UNEXPECTED REWARD

Healthy Revelation

*Fear the LORD, and turn away from evil. It will be healing
to your flesh and refreshment to your bones.*
PROVERBS 3:7–8 ESV

White sugar tastes good. It just does. I've never known a toddler who had to be taught to like ice cream. It just tastes good. But too much of it doesn't do good things to our bodies.

Honey, on the other hand, may not have the same appeal, but it has healthy rewards. The same goes for many natural substances the nutrition world urges us to include in our diets.

Eating right is a constant challenge because we are continually presented with options to the contrary. Billboards for fast-food chains abound. Vending machines are in every lobby. Our favorite coffee shops specialize in sugary drinks. Even the grocery aisles taunt us with tastes we remember fondly from childhood. These are not altogether bad choices, but they shouldn't be the norm. A diet of artificial ingredients and flavors does not promote good health.

Likewise, we need good spiritual nutrition to promote a strong spiritual life. Of course nothing compensates for reading God's Word; the Bread of Life provides essential nutrients. But after that, we must choose good supplements. Books that stimulate our minds to focus on Christ following and practical godly living are much better choices than fluffy, feel-good stories about angel visions and positive thinking. Not everything we read must be deep and complex, but our spiritual muscle can only grow in measure with the building blocks we give it. A personal trainer will tell you that whole foods are the best way to go. And the same can be said for our spiritual meals.

The writer of today's proverb reminds us that focusing on reverence for the Lord is spiritually healthy. And we will reap unexpected rewards from denying ourselves the cotton candy offered in the culture.

Often the true health of a person is revealed only when medical tests are done and the inner organs can be seen. That tells the tale of how hale and hearty the person is. The exterior may disguise what is really going on inside. And spiritually, we may appear vigorous and well, but when a spiritual test comes in the form of a temptation or trial, the real truth is revealed.

Today, choose to nurture your spiritual self in ways that will yield surprising rewards in the day of trials.

Dear God, thank You for Your Word. I want to nourish myself from its pages and be a healthy Christian. I open my heart to Your voice through it. Amen.

Startled by Scars

He heals the brokenhearted and binds up their wounds.
PSALM 147:3 ESV

Lord, take away this pain, please. Heal me.

Have you ever prayed a prayer like that?

Most of us have. The Bible tells us that Jesus healed people's bodies and spirits when He walked on this earth, and we know that God can heal our physical and emotional pain as well. Many prayer requests in church focus on healing. Lists of prayer requests are printed in bulletins. Stories of tragedies and requests for prayer are posted on social media.

God wants us to ask Him to intervene in our lives. But He also wants us to understand that healing comes in many ways. And we might be surprised at the way it comes to us.

God can heal instantly. And He does sometimes. We've heard the testimonies of those miraculously healed of cancer or some other terminal illness.

God can heal gradually. In these cases, He uses doctors and medications and therapies and time.

God can heal eternally. This is the answer we usually don't want, because it means the person has to leave this earth to receive healing.

But all three of these are healings. And what is sometimes just as surprising is the amazing beauty of the scars left behind.

Most of us don't think of scars as beauty marks. But God does. He sees in them the workings of His will in our lives. Our scars are ministry points, even if they are not outwardly visible. Emotional scars that have beautifully healed over become permanent memory moments that we can pull out and use to comfort someone else experiencing something similar.

And perhaps most importantly, Jesus has scars. His scars tell the story of His love for us. They are eternal marks of love.

Today if you're praying for healing, remember that it comes in different ways and that a scar is just the reminder of the love that bound up your wound.

Dear Lord, I have been wounded in life, and I bring my pain to You. Please bind up the battered places and heal me as You see best. Thank You for the beauty of scars. Amen.

Alien Beauty

These all died in faith, not having received the promises, but having seen them afar off were assured of them, embraced them and confessed that they were strangers and pilgrims on the earth.

HEBREWS 11:13 NKJV

A beautiful alien? What are you thinking of right now? Some scaly, silvery creature from a sci-fi special? Nope. That's not what we're going for here.

Alien beauty is what every woman of God wants to have. It's the best kind of beauty—eternal beauty.

Women today will find no shortage of beauty tips. But what is lacking is a sound philosophy to guide the use of the beauty tools. Trying to be beautiful for beauty's sake is not sufficient. Beauty is not and cannot be a stand-alone phenomenon. Beauty always reflects something or someone. We understand that beauty must be created. Artists, designers, chefs, musicians, landscapers, and architects are some of the creators of beauty in our world. And the beauty of humanity and nature is also the result of creation—God's.

Our human beauty creators may sign their work or copyright it or place it in a signature collection. It is known as theirs. They made it for a purpose; it reflects them, and they want it to be displayed in a particular way.

This is also true for our divine Creator. He designed and fashioned the beauty of women. They bear His signature. He wants their beauty displayed in a particular way. And to this world, that is an alien concept.

The self-promoting ideals of our world tell women to flaunt their assets and use their power. God says to surrender your power and steward your beauty; let it reflect His majesty. A woman who embraces this principle admits that the beauty of soul is what guides the beauty of body. She knows the truth of Proverbs 31:30 (NKJV): "Charm is deceitful and beauty is passing, but a woman who fears the LORD, she shall be praised."

Dear Father in heaven, I surrender my beauty to You. Guide me as I use it to reflect You, the Creator. Help me to embrace alien ideas here so that I may shine for You both on earth and in heaven. That is the real reward. Amen.

I Can't Stand My Relatives

*Miriam and Aaron spoke against Moses because of
the Cushite woman whom he had married.*
NUMBERS 12:1 ESV

All of us have prayed about an irritating person in our lives. But God puts them in contact with us for a reason. His purpose in giving us family is not so that we may be coddled and comforted but so that we will continue to grow in His likeness. Everything He allows in our lives is for that reason. In fact, when one is considering marriage, it is good to contemplate the idea that God is going to use this person not only to love me but to refine me. It might change our perspective on the conflicts we go through in marriage if we had that mind-set.

Moses' siblings had a problem with their sister-in-law. The Bible doesn't tell us just what it was, only that they spoke against him because of her. Perhaps they didn't like the fact that he had married a woman of another ethnicity. Perhaps they thought that her background as the daughter of a nomadic priest was unsuitable for the wife of the deliverer (see Exodus 2:16, 21). Maybe they just didn't get along with her personality; maybe they didn't like the way she cooked. We don't know. But it was something that they weren't letting fade away.

God dealt with them severely because of their mistreatment of Moses. In Bible times, judgment was usually swift and severe. Today, in the dispensation of grace, God doesn't strike us with leprosy like He did Miriam (Numbers 12:10). But He does want us to get along with the people around us and those in our families.

A surprising thing might happen when we pray about our familial relationships, though. God probably won't remove our family members from our lives, but He will give us the power we need to get along with them and even to discover things we can like about them.

You see, most often it's our selfishness that gets in the way. We like people to conform to our ideas and opinions. Growing close to someone who doesn't like what we like is difficult. But that's where grace comes in, and it's available to us now!

Dear Lord, I've been praying about the difficult person in my family, but I've just been asking You to fix her [him] and not acknowledging that I need to change too. Do Your work in me, and help me to love her [him]. In the name of Jesus, amen.

Dead Things That Live

"Truly, truly, I say to you, unless a grain of wheat falls into the earth and dies, it remains alone; but if it dies, it bears much fruit."
JOHN 12:24 ESV

When I plant my garden in the spring, I am eager for the first green shoots to poke through the ground. I know something is happening under the soil, but I can't wait to see the evidence. I walk down the rows, leaning down and peering intently at the dirt, hoping to see even the tiniest glimmer of life. But it takes awhile.

Under the cover of the dark earth, a seed is rotting and dying, its cellular structure being broken down by the loamy chemicals in its garden bed. As it dies, it disintegrates until it doesn't even resemble what was interred. Then slowly it takes on a different composition, and something begins to happen in the heart of that seed. The spark of life that has always been there starts to expand and push away the layers of sod. And one day, up into the light, a seedling raises its head.

We don't usually expect life to come from death. We expect morgues to hold lifeless forms, landfills to contain refuse, and junkyards to harbor crashed vehicles. If bodies walked around and garbage became delicious and wrecks morphed into drivable form, we'd feel spooked. And rightly so. The principle of death is at work in every aspect of our world.

But the principle of life is also present. And Jesus said death, in His hands, springs into life. "I am the resurrection and the life. Whoever believes in me, though he die, yet shall he live" (John 11:25 ESV). For there to be a resurrection, there must first be a death.

From the world's perspective, funerals are the end of life. But from God's view, they are the beginning. This is the unexpected power of life that we can claim as believers. And it works in whatever particular spiritual crisis you are facing today. From the death of your will comes the life of His Spirit in you. He has promised. Embrace death, and life will spring forth.

Lord Jesus, You are the Resurrection. You are life. Today, I bring to You the dead things that I cannot make live again. I ask You to bring new life from them through Your mighty power. Amen.

Trying to Save the Temporal

They exchanged the truth about God for a lie and worshiped and served the creature rather than the Creator, who is blessed forever! Amen.

ROMANS 1:25 ESV

"Hug a tree."

"Save the whales."

"Go green."

All these slogans remind us of our God-given commission to steward the earth He created. The resources in it are gifts, and we must use them thankfully and responsibly. Nature and animal life are to be protected and cared for, but they are not to be elevated to a status God didn't intend for them to have.

It's true that human beings tend to be slothful and sloppy, and we need reminders not to take advantage of our beautiful habitat. There is certainly nothing wrong with planting trees, protecting our waterways, and recycling plastic and paper to cut down on landfill waste. The problem arises when we believe that our planet's longevity depends on us or that we cannot ever cut down a tree or use an animal for food.

In Genesis 1:28 (ESV), God gave Adam and Eve instructions about the world He had made for them: "God blessed them. And God said to them, 'Be fruitful and multiply and fill the earth and subdue it, and have dominion over the fish of the sea and over the birds of the heavens and over every living thing that moves on the earth.' "

The first couple was instructed by the Creator to oversee the earth and its creatures and even to subdue and have dominion over creation. We know from Genesis 1:27 that man was different from the animals, because God breathed His very own eternal breath into his nostrils. And this verse concurs with that by telling us that man and woman are of a higher order than nature and have the responsibility to rule it well.

The apostle Peter reminded us that this earth and all that is in it is temporary: "All flesh is like grass and all its glory like the flower of grass. The grass withers, and the flower falls" (1 Peter 1:24 ESV).

We are not to spend our highest energy on the natural world, which will fade and someday be burned up. Instead, we are to spend our greatest efforts on what is eternal—people. Loving the natural world is good and right so long as it falls into its proper place under love for the humans for which God gave His Son. Don't hug trees; hug people.

Heavenly Father, I love the beautiful world You created. I want to be a good steward of its resources, so help me keep that in proper balance with the love I need to show for people. Amen.

The Surprising Order

For man was not made from woman, but woman from man.
1 CORINTHIANS 11:8 ESV

When the great ship *Titanic* was going down on the night of April 15, 1912, Captain E. J. Smith gave the orders to put women and children on the lifeboats. It was slow work. The ship was barely listing to the side and seemed secure. The lifeboats dangling over the side on their davits looked flimsy and unsafe. Women didn't want to leave their husbands. The poorly trained crew lowered many of the lifeboats into the water with less than their capacity. But among the souls who did escape in them were a few men, some of them disguised in some way or trying not to be noticed. This was a rather shameful fact in days to come.

If a similar situation were to occur today, I wonder if those aboard would protest the chivalrous code of women and children first. Somehow, I believe, in moments of crisis, that we realize, no matter what our opinions elsewhere, that the heart of men to protect women is a noble thing, a God-given impulse.

Men were designed with the beat of testosterone in their veins, a rhythm that inclines them to adventure and to risk but also to defend what is precious and vulnerable. While this is denigrated in many ways in modern culture, it is nonetheless true biologically as well as socially. You will be hard pressed to find a setting where men will not try to surround the women if disaster approaches. It is written into their DNA.

So when women attempt to change the order, the outcome is usually negative. Try to imagine the women aboard the *Titanic* insisting that the men go first. Impossible. Our imaginations can't even conjure up such a scene—pregnant Madeleine Astor making her husband take her place, and other women watching their men wave to them from the lifeboats while they flounder in the icy water. *No,* our minds scream. *That's not right.*

The unexpectedness of God's way of doing things is beautiful. Modern man thinks he can improve it, but the attempts to do so sadly give no satisfaction, no completion. Woman was made from man, and in his very soul, man recognizes his responsibility to nurture and protect. Perhaps that was why Martin Luther called his wife, Katherine, "Kitty, my rib."

May we celebrate the surprising beauty of following the great mind of our Creator. There is unexpected power for all of us in that.

Father God, You created us in Your image and designed how we relate to one another. Help me today to be grateful for the amazing contribution men make and to honor the plan You put in place. Amen.

Startling Deliverance

By faith Moses, when he was born, was hidden for three months
by his parents, because they saw that the child was beautiful,
and they were not afraid of the king's edict.

Hebrews 11:23 ESV

It was a terrible time to have a new baby. The life of a slave laborer was hard and gave little time for mothering. Moreover, the pharaoh had ordered all infant boys to be killed. Nevertheless, Jochebed gave birth to a beautiful baby boy. The midwives were on her side and refused to toss him into the Nile. And so the family hid him for as long as they could, until one day they had to make other arrangements.

Whose idea it was to float him in a basket in the river, we don't know. But surely no weaver ever worked more carefully than Jochebed as she made his floating bed and waterproofed it with pitch. Maybe she had to work on it at night when her other labors were over. Maybe she huddled in a corner, trying to hide the light as she kept at her task. But she was resolute in her decision and calm in her attitude. She and her husband were not afraid of the king who held their lives at his disposal. They trusted in Jehovah, whose care reached further than any earthly monarch.

Did Jochebed know that the princess went to the river to bathe? Did she intend for Moses to be found? It's very possible. She stationed her daughter there as a sentinel, to keep tabs on what happened. Miriam had probably been instructed in what to say, but who could have guessed that it would turn out so beautifully? The new life that endangered them all became the source of their deliverance.

What new thing has God brought into your life that seems negative and dangerous? What is He telling you to do to help His plan go forward? Weave a basket? Stand guard?

Step out in faith and do it. Deliverance comes in unexpected ways.

Dear Father, thank You for the surprising ways You bring deliverance to our world. Help me follow what You have for me to do today. In Jesus' name, amen.

The Wonder of Forgetfulness

The chief cupbearer did not remember Joseph, but forgot him.
GENESIS 40:23 ESV

Generally, forgetfulness is not a positive trait. I am not naturally good at remembering names, and I have to make it a point to use a name two or three times after I hear it to keep it in my mind associated with the person.

Forgetfulness seems to get worse as one ages. Jokes abound about "senior moments" and walking into a room and not remembering why. Those with certain diseases and conditions also struggle with forgetfulness. In any case, I don't believe I've ever heard anyone refer to forgetfulness as a blessing. But it was for Joseph, though he didn't realize it at the time.

You remember the account of Joseph—favored son, hated brother, was sold into slavery, became chief servant, was lied about and thrown into prison, interpreted dreams. Now he waited. The king's cupbearer, who was happily serving the throne again, did not even remember the man whose interpretation had foretold his good fortune.

This had to be God at work. If the cupbearer had told Pharaoh about Joseph as soon as he had been restored, there would have been no crisis to cause the ruler to need Joseph's release from prison. God made the cupbearer forget for two long years. Then, when the king was greatly disturbed by a dream that none of his advisers could interpret, the man remembered. It was time. Joseph was needed, and the pharaoh was so upset he was willing to listen to a prisoner who could help him.

At times in our lives, others forget or we forget. Sometimes we feel like God has forgotten. We see ways that things could work out. Surely

Joseph did too as he passed day after day in the prison, going about his routines, wondering if today might be the day his name would be called and he would be summoned. Surely he was tempted to despair as month rolled into month and one year into two. But God had not forgotten him, and the moment of release had already been planned in His calendar.

So it is with us. Don't give in to Satan's lies. Never doubt that God is at work every second, every minute, every day, every month, every year. What looks like a curse may instead be a blessing. God remembers you, and at the right time, release will come.

Dear heavenly Father, I know I can trust You just like Joseph did. You were with him, and You will be with me. Thank You for watching over everything that concerns me. Amen.

Rescued in the Wilderness

*So she called the name of the L*ORD *who spoke to her,*
"You are a God of seeing," for she said, "Truly here
I have seen him who looks after me."
GENESIS 16:13 ESV

Pregnant, homeless and alone, Hagar was lying beside a spring in the wilderness. What an unexpected life she'd had. The Bible tells us that she was an Egyptian, likely a present to Abraham's household when the king gave him gifts to get him to leave after he lied about Sarah. As a slave, she'd never had a say in her own life. She had a mistress in Egypt; she had a mistress in Sarah. She did what she was told. When Sarah told her they were going to observe the custom of the handmaiden bearing a child for her mistress, we don't know what she thought. Probably she realized that bearing a child would assure her of better circumstances for as long as she lived. As the mother of the child of a great man like Abraham, she would receive better treatment for her son's sake. Women in that time were not given much consideration, especially if they were of the servant class, so this was maybe her only hope of bettering her station in life.

As for the way it would affect her standing with Abraham, it was a common practice in those days and didn't signify anything other than a type of surrogate motherhood for the chief wife. Abraham was an old man; she was merely the means to an heir.

But when it became apparent that she had conceived a child, Hagar's chance for a better life went to her head. She, the lowly slave, had achieved something the beloved Sarah had not. She was fertile; Sarah was barren. The girl who had never had anything to boast of suddenly realized her leverage. And that was her downfall.

Now she lay disheveled in the desert, thinking she and the unborn baby would die. She'd been better off as she was before. At least she'd be alive.

But God had other plans. He didn't want Abraham and Sarah to interfere with His timetable, but He'd allowed them the free will to do it anyway. And He came to the aid of the girl caught in the middle.

What are you facing in your wilderness? Whose interference has changed the course of your life? What plans have been rearranged?

Look up. The angel may be hovering near. You are loved by the "God who sees."

Father, You see me just as You saw Hagar. Thank You for being in my wilderness. Help me trust Your work in my life. Amen.

Unplanned but Redeemed

Behold, children are a heritage from the LORD,
the fruit of the womb a reward.
PSALM 127:3 ESV

If you say the word *unplanned*, *pregnancy* seems to go with it. We've grown accustomed to the partnering of those two ideas, but God's Word tells us that His plans are different from ours.

I don't understand how the union of an unmarried couple that produces a child can fit into the blessing of this verse, but that's not for me to figure out. The will of God redeems more situations than I could imagine with my human brain. And the sovereignty of God covers more possibilities than I can sort through. What I do know is that children are His to give.

When I worked as a volunteer counselor in a crisis pregnancy center, we were known as a place with free pregnancy tests. We regularly received clients who were frightened about the possibility of being pregnant, most of them in unstable situations. The idea of a baby was not welcome; rather, it brought up emotions of anxiety, fear, and confusion.

The Bible tells us the story of one unplanned child, a little boy conceived in an affair between King David and Bathsheba, the wife of one of his military men. Her pregnancy, the boy's life, was David's motivation for scheming the death of her husband and covering his own sin. The little boy's life was short, but his impact on his father was great. David wept and prayed for him.

More often the Bible tells the stories of barren women who longed for children. In ancient times, children were the way a woman was assured of future care and present respect.

Today women often have ambivalent feelings about children: we want them, but on our schedule. The awful genocide of abortion has cut a bloody swath through the generations, robbing us of the lives and legacies of precious millions. God is gracious and merciful, but there is a price to pay for so callously disregarding the heritage of the Lord.

If you are experiencing an unplanned pregnancy or know someone who is, remember that blessings come in unusual packages. Don't discount the reward to be received in accepting the surprise of a life that is unexpected on earth but planned in God's heart.

Father God, there are no surprise babies in Your sight. You see the beginning of them all and redeem their origins out of Your great love. Help me to cherish children always as Your reward. In Jesus' name, amen.

Rewards of Ministry

Now there was in Joppa a disciple named Tabitha, which, translated, means Dorcas. She was full of good works and acts of charity.

ACTS 9:36 ESV

Have you ever known a woman whose whole life was devoted to cheerfully serving others? If you have, you've been blessed just to be around her.

I'm thinking of some women I've known who have the gift of blessing others with their cooking, their sewing machines, their cleaning abilities, their helpfulness. Sometimes they're very quiet about it and you don't really realize how large a contribution they make until they're gone.

That was the case with Dorcas. She lived in the city of Joppa and was an important part of the church there. In fact, she had a closet ministry. She helped fill the closets of widows in need of clothing. The Bible tells us that she was full of charitable works. When she suddenly took ill and died, her church family was stunned, shocked, bereaved. And did they ever miss her smiling face and helpful hands!

God allowed the apostle Peter to raise her back to life in the name of Jesus, and no doubt her ministry continued on without a hitch. When you're called, you're called. She could not stop doing what was in her heart to do.

You may be involved in some type of ministry that feels like a dead end. It can be that way sometimes. We don't always see the widows' gratefulness. Sometimes the hours are long. It feels like we're in a tiny corner of the world by ourselves. We're not seeing the results we'd imagined.

Don't give up. Like Dorcas, you may be contributing far more than you know. The little acts of kindness you do every day matter to the ones who receive them. And the ministry in which you're involved would do less if you weren't part of it.

When Dorcas died, the church sent two men right away to get the apostle. They weren't content to be without her. They knew they needed her gifts and presence. And your church needs you too!

Refuse the lies of Satan that your contributions don't matter. Go sew a tunic today! (Or the twenty-first-century equivalent!)

Father, I know I have an important part to play in the ministry of my church. Help me fill my spot today with enthusiasm and excellence like Dorcas did. Amen.

Rewards of Willingness

One who heard us was a woman named Lydia, from the city of
Thyatira, a seller of purple goods, who was a worshiper of God.
The Lord opened her heart to pay attention to what was said
by Paul. And after she was baptized, and her household as
well, she urged us, saying, "If you have judged me to be
faithful to the Lord, come to my house and stay."
ACTS 16:14–15 ESV

Lydia was probably a wealthy businesswoman. No doubt she had a
spacious, well-appointed house. And she was willing to share it.

In their travels, Paul and Silas met believers on the Sabbath by the
river in the town of Philippi. The Christians in those days often had no
buildings to use and may even have chosen to meet in a place where
they wouldn't attract attention since the practice of Christianity was
often squelched and the cause of persecution. Paul and Silas would
meet with the local members of the body and encourage them and
stay as long as they could to help establish them.

In this particular town, there was a group of women who met for
prayer. The missionaries met with them, and afterward this woman
named Lydia approached them with a request. She asked them to
stay with her while they were in the area. She opened her home as a
base of operations and probably as a source of spiritual enrichment to
her household, since the Bible tells us that all of them had just been
baptized as proof of their faith in Christ.

The story that follows is the account of the slave girl whose demons
were exorcised and whose master then had Paul and Silas thrown into
prison, with their feet fastened in stocks. After their midnight praise

service and the earthquake God sent, there was a revival in the jail and the jailer and his family came to faith in Jesus.

Would this have happened had Lydia not allowed the missionaries to use her home? We don't know.

We do know that a willingness to share what we have results in rewards. At times I have been reluctant to share my home or my resources or my time. You have probably had those times as well—for a variety of reasons, not all of them selfish. But when we make the sacrifice and open up our palms in good ways, God can take the blessings we have and bring others to Him.

Dear Lord, I don't have the resources Lydia had, but I do have something. Help me to recognize when I need to offer help, and give me a willing heart. In the name of Jesus, amen.

Rewards of Training

I long to see you, that I may be filled with joy. I am reminded of your sincere faith, a faith that dwelt first in your grandmother Lois and your mother Eunice and now, I am sure, dwells in you as well.

2 TIMOTHY 1:4–5 ESV

Parenting is a job with the big picture in view as well as a focus on today.

Many of the things we do today as moms seem like an endless repetition of yesterday and the day before. We say the same things, do the same things, discipline for the same things, and so on. How easy it is to forget that all of these little building blocks are creating a gigantic masterpiece.

The apostle Paul took joy in his spiritual son Timothy. But he recognized that the faith that was in him was the result of two women who had played a foundational role in his upbringing—his mother and grandmother. Since Timothy's father is never mentioned in Paul's writings, many scholars believe he was an unbeliever, probably a Greek man. But the women are mentioned as the ones who helped establish the young Timothy in the way of Christ. They had a sincere faith. And their training was rewarded in the young man who became Paul's protégé and blessed others through his own ministry.

Parenting seeks to establish ground rules on which other principles can be laid. It is not necessary that children understand all the intricacies of the boundaries as long as they know enough to obey. In other words, it is impossible to explain everything to a toddler, but that will come as he or she gets older. For now, there are some basics.

- Perseverance: don't quit.
- Commitment: do what you say.

- Kindness: be helpful in every situation.
- Respect: don't disregard authority.
- Truth: don't lie.
- Gratefulness: say thank you.

These are just a few of the things we can teach from early ages. The fine points of the concepts will come later, but we can first require the behavior, which will lay the foundation for future reward.

I don't know how Eunice raised her little son, Timothy, but I know she taught him enough that he was a well-rounded, believing young man when he came into contact with the apostle Paul. Let's teach our own children well and encourage other moms as they mold the future world changers they have in their kitchens today.

Heavenly Father, You give children to us to raise. Guide our minds and hearts as we lay the foundation so that You can use them in the future. In Jesus' name, amen.

Rewards of Submission

Then Mary said, "Behold the maidservant of the Lord!
Let it be to me according to your word."
LUKE 1:38 NKJV

Perhaps no woman in history has been talked about more than Mary, the mother of Jesus. By her own words, she acknowledged that people of every generation would call her blessed. What a privilege to give birth to the Messiah! And it came as a reward for her attitude of submission.

We know the story very well. Mary was a small-town girl, a virgin betrothed to a carpenter. One day an angel appeared to her, and everything in her world changed. Much has been written and sung about her and Joseph and their journey to Bethlehem. Some have even talked about the shame she endured and the stigma under which she probably lived her life. But we need to highlight her submission.

Did Mary have a choice? Yes. Every human being, even the chosen mother of Christ, has free will. It seems she could have refused this assignment from heaven. She could have used her confusion as an excuse or declined because of the awkwardness of explaining it to family members. She could have said no to the privilege of feeling His life inside her and being the first person on earth to know He was coming. She could have declined to go through the embarrassment of being pregnant before her wedding. She could have rejected all the joy and all the pain. But she didn't. Mary said yes. She said, "Let it be." She submitted her desires and her plans to One greater. And she didn't even know how it would all turn out! We can read the rest of the story; she couldn't.

Submission to God is a sign of true faith, of trust. It shows our heart of obedience toward Him. Many today are afraid to submit. Perhaps they have been taken advantage of by someone in power; maybe they have been brought up with the lie that you shouldn't bow to anyone or anything—do life your way. Either of these attitudes can damage our understanding.

But the God who asked Mary to give birth to Jesus is in charge of our lives as well. And He asks us to submit to His plan for us, not to harm us, but to love us through it.

*Dear Father, thank You for sending Your Son to this earth.
Thank You for Mary's submission. I want to follow her
example and see the wonderful rewards in my
own life as I surrender my will to You. Amen.*

Rewards of Faith

Now there was one, Anna, a prophetess, the daughter of Phanuel,
of the tribe of Asher. She was of a great age, and had lived with
a husband seven years from her virginity; and this woman was a
widow of about eighty-four years, who did not depart from the
temple, but served God with fastings and prayers night and day.
And coming in that instant she gave thanks to the Lord, and spoke
of Him to all those who looked for redemption in Jerusalem.
LUKE 2:36–38 NKJV

I remember the nine months of waiting for my children to be born. I often experienced nausea and tiredness in the first trimester, but after that, every week was exciting as the time of birth drew nearer. Toward the end, I got really tired of waiting. Every pregnancy seemed to lag as the final days approached. I wanted more than anything to see their little faces and have them in my arms and not in my belly!

Imagine waiting a lifetime for a child! That's what Anna had done. She was eighty-four years old on the day when Joseph and Mary brought the infant Jesus to the temple to present Him to God in a special ceremony. She was a widow whose husband didn't live very long after their marriage, but we're not sure if she had any children of her own. We do know, however, that she was expecting the coming of the Messiah.

Luke's account tells us that Anna served God continually in the temple, night and day, with fasting and prayer. That is dedication! Perhaps she didn't want to miss the promise. Perhaps she couldn't bear the thought of being absent on the day when the Christ child appeared. So she came continually. And she waited and had faith, through days and months and years.

A woman's life is filled with seasons of waiting. Some of them are easier to endure than others. But having faith while we wait is challenging. Days turn into weeks, and it seems our prayers are unanswered and our hopes are for nothing. Remember Anna. Remember her faith. Remember her reward. Yours may come just as unexpectedly.

Dear heavenly Father, as I wait in faith, help me hold to Your promise and never let it go. I rejoice in You today. Amen.

Rewards of Tears

Those who sow in tears shall reap in joy. He who continually goes forth weeping, bearing seed for sowing, shall doubtless come again with rejoicing, bringing his sheaves with him.

PSALM 126:5–6 NKJV

Tears are an investment.

As a farmer sows seeds in the ground, investing for a harvest of grain, so a Christian sows tears of determination, investing for a harvest of souls.

Gardening is the oldest job—the first job—on earth. Adam and Eve, the first couple, were assigned to tend the garden of Eden even before sin entered the world. Work preceded sin. God created us to be purposeful and useful. It is intriguing to me that the job He gave them was working with the botanical life He had created. He knew it was good for them. And I think gardening is good for us today. Working with the soil and seeing things grow, tending to the beauty of flowers and vegetables and herbs, harvesting the bounty He produces—these are activities that cause us to be more balanced and content. In fact, according to some study I read about, farmers are the happiest people on earth. I believe it. Working God's earth has that effect.

Sowing tears for the spiritual well-being of others is like gardening. We see the barren ground of their souls, and we tenderly work the ground and pray over it and share the precious seed of the Word of God whenever we can. Then we hover over it and watch as God uses other people and events to water the seed in their lives. We stand by with joy as little signs of spiritual life begin to appear. We are thrilled to see blossoms and growth. And finally, one day, we rejoice in the full harvest of a life committed to Christ. And that person goes on to repeat the cycle.

We don't hear a lot about soul winning, but it is still very close to God's heart. Proverbs 11:30 tells us that whoever wins souls "is wise." God wants all the people of the earth to know about His love for them and His plan to redeem them. You and I need to be open to being "tear sowers." There is no greater joy than seeing a new life in Christ begin.

Dear God, You are not willing that anyone perish in eternity without You. Today, show me how I can sow in tears and reap in the joy of a soul harvest for You. Amen.

Rewards of Doing Good

Let us not grow weary of doing good,
for in due season we will reap, if we do not give up.
GALATIANS 6:9 ESV

When my children were little, there were things I taught them to do for the express purpose of doing good. One example was making their beds. Some parents use a system of rewards for everything a child is required to do. I did use chore charts for a while. But my overall opinion came to be that my children needed to learn to do some things without a reward, at least for a tangible reward like money or candy or time on a screened device. They needed to do good for the reward of doing good.

As adults, no one rewards us with stickers or extra allowance if we make our beds and straighten our rooms and put away the dishes on the counter. These things are just part of being a responsible adult and living in a tidy house. My mother used to encourage me to relish the "feeling of accomplishment" that came from cleaning the house or clearing the sink of dishes. I believe she was onto something there. And I tried to instill that in my children. Some things we do just because they need to be done, and that's reward enough.

In a spiritual realm, there are some things we need to do just for the sake of doing good.

- Attending corporate worship with other believers
- Spending personal worship time with Jesus
- Giving back the tithe to God and supporting the church
- Fellowshipping with other believers outside of service
- Giving to missions and praying for missionaries

- Going to additional church conferences and functions

These things we should do because they are right and good for us.

In the bustle of life, it is tempting to slack off on church attendance or other means of intentional spiritual enrichment. Let me encourage you in the words of the apostle Paul not to let that happen. Don't get weary with doing good things. The basics are necessary. And for doing them, you will reap rewards that far outweigh any inconvenience or feeling of monotony; you will reap eternal blessings.

Dear Lord, please give me a persevering spirit and help me not to despise the routine of doing good that keeps me grounded and spiritually healthy. Amen.

Rewards of Time

Look carefully then how you walk, not as unwise but as wise,
making the best use of the time, because the days are evil.
EPHESIANS 5:15–16 ESV

My college choir director was a dynamo of energy. His accomplishments at my alma mater are legendary. He gave and gave of time and energy and money. He had a relentless passion to see the music department advance and a boundless vision for the future. He also knew how to use time.

I recall how he would make use of even five minutes left in rehearsal. Instead of letting us leave early, he'd call out the name of another composition, and we'd begin hammering out a few notes before the bell rang. He used what I have called "corners of time."

We all have them—the little bits of time in and around our main events of the day—fifteen minutes here, five minutes there. Before an appointment, in between clients—time in the hourglass that goes unused.

If we would learn to use our corners, we could accomplish some big things in little bits. It's the idea some of our grandmothers had when they routinely took their knitting bags with them. Whenever they had a few minutes to spare, they'd pull out a knitting project and get a few more stitches in. Ever so slowly, they'd finish sweaters and socks and scarves. We can learn from their example. Our bags might contain different kinds of projects, but we might update an address book, read a chapter in a book, or pen a note to someone we care about.

In a spiritual sense, we need to make use of the corners of time, because every bit of it is a gift from God, a trust we must steward well. We must not just spend time making our own lives better; we should be looking around for the good we can do for others, especially as it relates to ministering to the needs of their souls.

It's amazing how much one can accomplish in a little bit of time. Let's do it today.

Dear Father, thank You for the gift of time. I have twenty-four hours in my day just like everyone else. Help me to use those hours wisely and well. In the name of Jesus, amen.

Significance

An excellent wife who can find?
She is far more precious than jewels.
PROVERBS 31:10 ESV

If there is any theme that is relevant to every person in every generation, it is the idea of significance. All of us want to know we matter. We want to believe that our lives make a difference, that our lives will leave some small mark.

Culture recognizes this search for significance. Books, seminars, and therapies for self-image, self-actualization, and mindful living are boundless. Counselors and therapists try to help their forlorn clients battle their way through the maze of internal and external factors that pull them down.

As followers of Christ, we know that our significance comes from being in relationship with Him. We know we are valuable twice—He created us and He redeemed us. Regardless of our past, our abilities, our stories, or our flaws, we have worth to Him. And our future is secured in Him.

Still, we are not immune to the messages that come at us from our own self-doubts as well as from the enemy. And so it is good to remind ourselves of truth. There we find our balance.

The writer of Proverbs 31 knew that women who embrace their calling in God's world are precious. A woman who understands that all of us are created for a beautiful, specific purpose can then delight in filling it.

My oldest daughter is called to be a nurse. God has gifted her with the temperament and abilities she needs to accomplish that. I am thrilled to see her discover joy in that career. Yet I have often told my daughters that if God brings a special man into their lives and they choose to marry, they must be willing to subordinate their careers to the higher calling of wife and possibly mother. This doesn't mean that a woman can't continue to find fulfillment in a profession or ministry, but she should never elevate that above her calling in the home, which is more precious than jewels. I believe the reason many women feel fragmented and discontented is that we have not been taught to realize the fundamental delight that accompanies being a woman in the home first and then letting other pursuits fill in the gaps. But this is what the wisest man on earth wrote down for our benefit. And it's more than a nice verse to be read on Mother's Day. It's a principle we should take to heart as we search for that significant place God has for every woman.

Creator God, You made me a woman. I delight in that calling and in my abilities to create a home, if that is Your plan for me. Help me to major on what You do and let my focus be to glorify You in every part of my life. In Jesus' name, amen.

Trust

The heart of her husband trusts in her, and he will have no lack of gain. She does him good, and not harm, all the days of her life.
<small>PROVERBS 31:11–12 ESV</small>

Trust is one of those basic building blocks of relationship. It's almost impossible to have a meaningful relationship without it. A woman who cultivates the trust of her husband is a wise woman.

The Bible has a lot to say about women who are destructive. Some translations call her the "strange woman." Others refer to her as the "immoral woman." Here are some of her attributes:

- Flatters with her words. Proverbs 2:16
- Practices deceit. Proverbs 5:3
- Forsakes the husband of her youth. Proverbs 2:17
- Forgets the covenant of her God. Proverbs 2:17
- Keeps those who go to her from returning. Proverbs 2:19
- Seduces with her eyes. Proverbs 6:25
- Reduces men to a crust of bread. Proverbs 6:26
- Preys on precious life. Proverbs 6:26
- Destroys strong men. Proverbs 7:26
- Makes her house the way to hell. Proverbs 7:27

This is the kind of woman who cannot be trusted. She uses deceit, flattery, seduction, and manipulation. She is a black widow kind of woman, who uses a man for her purposes and then destroys him.

But the woman God celebrates is one who invites her husband's trust in her. She is good for him and does good to him. She will not bring harm to him. He can trust her every day of his life.

Since the garden of Eden, Satan has appealed to women's pride to get them to use their power over their husbands. And in our culture today, that approach is still prevalent. The growing disdain for distinct masculinity is distorting our view of the relationship between good men and good women.

We must cling to this ancient text inspired by God. The godly woman invites trust and lives up to it. That's a power that is rare and wonderful.

Father, I want to be a woman who can be trusted by the good men in my life. Empower me to live in truth and to be a safe place for my husband. In Jesus' name, amen.

Willingness

She seeks wool and flax, and works with willing hands.
PROVERBS 31:13 ESV

Once we moved into a house that had been rented by college girls. It was a spacious two-story home with wooden floors and long windows, sunny rooms and vintage appeal. But it had housed women who were not willing workers. In fact, they were quite the opposite.

The state of the house was appalling—clothes in heaps, a stench throughout, and sinks that needed to be burned out in order to sterilize them. It was incredible that women actually had been the tenants. It would have been easier to believe that a group of sloppy children had been hiding out.

Being willing to work and to seek out useful work is an important aspect of godly womanhood. God made us to reflect His image, and He is a being of order and beauty.

In the beginning, the earth was formless (Genesis 1:2). God made it beautiful. We are told that God does not author confusion (1 Corinthians 14:33). He likes order.

Of course, people have different standards when it comes to housekeeping, but a general sense of cleanliness and order is a great gift a woman can bring to her environment. The term *a woman's touch* should still mean something.

Is there a spiritual aspect to this idea of being a willing worker in our study of womanhood?

Yes, if we consider the idea that Jesus came to serve others willingly. Maybe the wording in Philippians 2:7 where Jesus took on the "form of a servant" could be translated "He took the towel of a servant."

Perhaps it is a reference to His willing and voluntary act of washing the disciples' feet at the Last Supper. If our Lord can do menial tasks and glorify the Father through His service, so can we!

Lord Jesus, give me today a heart that is willing to work and willing to serve. Thank You for being willing to humble Yourself. I want to be like You. Amen.

Inspiration

She is like the ships of the merchant;
she brings her food from afar.
PROVERBS 31:14 ESV

In ancient times, merchants brought the glories of trade to other lands. There were no supermarkets or chain stores. There was no online retail. Everything was brought by ship, carefully packed and preserved. Cargo on merchant ships was precious. If it was lost, both the shipping company and the merchant suffered loss. This is why it was such a big deal that the mariners tossed the goods on their ship into the sea when God sent a storm after Jonah (see Jonah 1:5).

When the biblical author wrote Proverbs 31 about womanhood, he knew about merchant trade. He was very well acquainted with what items were imported from faraway places. There were spices from the Orient and citrus from the islands, silk from Persia and cotton from Egypt. And he envisioned this woman as an adventurer, bringing delight to the senses of her family with the wonderful way she prepared their meals and kept their home.

The closest I ever got to exotic trade was in the marketplace in Juarez, Mexico. I enjoyed the banter and the colorful sights and the bustle of many people, but I was a very inexperienced shopper in that kind of setting. The merchants likely got more of my money than they should have. But this Proverbs woman knew how to gather resources for her home that inspired the people she loved.

What about you?

Sometimes we forget to lay out the meat to thaw or realize we don't have the right ingredients for the special dessert. We may even have to substitute a quick carryout pizza for dinner. Life happens like that sometimes. The heart of the matter is that we can be more than a galley cook to those in our homes. We can provide inspiration for their days by the way we nourish their senses through normal, everyday things like food.

Dear God, this is a challenging part of the description of a godly woman. Help me apply this to my life in a positive way so I can inspire those in my home. Amen.

Industry

*She rises while it is yet night and provides food
for her household and portions for her maidens.*
PROVERBS 31:15 ESV

My dear mother-in-law believed in a literal application of Proverbs 31:15. For as long as I knew her, up until she became very ill with stage 4 cancer, she would get up at 5:00 in the morning to start her day. She wanted to follow this scripture about getting up while it is still night. And for me, 5:00 a.m. is still very much night! I really admired her dedication to this practice, though I'm afraid I didn't join her in it. She would get up and have her private worship time with the Lord and then get dressed and tidy up the house before anyone else got up. I have to admit it sounds like a good plan. But alas, I have not, as yet, implemented it.

Many women do get up rather early to start their day. Some have children to dress and drop off at school before work. Others have to start homeschooling. Still others are caregivers for aging parents or have other early morning responsibilities. And let's not forget stay-at-home mothers of toddlers who are never allowed a wink of sleep past 7:00! To a preschooler, that's practically sleeping in!

God's Word shows us its practicality in Proverbs 31. The virtuous woman is commended for being diligent and industrious. Not only does she take care of her family, but also her staff. *What? Staff?*

Most of us don't have servants. We wouldn't know what to do with them if we did, though most of us would like to give them a try! But remember that having servants means more to do in some ways, since one must keep them employed and fed and instructed in what to do.

So I'll just settle for the household I have. I may never be quite as disciplined as my mother-in-law, but I hope that my children will remember that I was diligent about taking care of my family's daily needs. I know you do too.

Father, I want to honor You in the way I start and end my day.
I pray that You would empower me to do this well. Amen.

Resourcefulness

She considers a field and buys it;
with the fruit of her hands she plants a vineyard.
PROVERBS 31:16 ESV

One of the things I recall about living near Ohio's Amish country was the skill of the women in tending their flower beds. Our family enjoyed spending a summer evening driving through the countryside, up the little lanes and down through homey villages. We would see Amish men at work in their fields with teams of horses, Amish teen girls on bicycles running errands in town, Amish children in their miniature garb, and Amish women busy in their flowers.

While men took care of growing things in the fields, the flowers around the house and in the yard were the pride and joy of the women. I've not seen many hanging baskets that compare with the gorgeous blooms they had. And beside their porches and by their trees and wherever else they could grow them were neat rows of beautiful flowers. These women who lived a Plain life in many respects had great appreciation for beauty, and it showed.

Contrast this with the story in the Bible about Jezebel, who confiscated the vineyard of a man named Naboth and had him killed so she could give the place to her whining husband. That's the exact opposite of the trait God's Word commends.

It seems as though this woman described in Proverbs 31 had an understanding of real estate and property values. She had the knowledge and the skill to buy a field and then to plant her own vineyard. She had learned how to be resourceful, and everyone around her reaped the benefit of it.

God has given you the opportunity to be resourceful. It may not be in the area of property, but there are ways you can bless your home and family that you may not have considered yet. If you are married, your husband shouldn't be left wondering about your activities, but you should let him know your skills and discuss how they could benefit everyone.

This woman in Proverbs embodied impressive skills, but so do you. You just may need to uncover them and polish them up a bit. You never know what may happen when you do!

Dear God, help me discover how my gifts and skills can benefit my family. I know that I enjoy _____. Show me if this is something I can use in a way I hadn't already considered. Amen.

Strength

She dresses herself with strength and makes her arms strong.
PROVERBS 31:17 ESV

A lot is said today about a woman being strong and brave. But God originated that idea in millennia past.

Around the turn of the twentieth century, women began to revolt in cultural ways. They marched for the right to vote. They demanded the right to wear trousers and cut their hair short. They insisted on freedom from sexual restraints; "petting parties" became popular, and contraception came about as a way to liberate women from the consequence of pregnancy. They took up smoking, which traditionally had been a male pursuit. They were known as "flappers." They began to look for ways to prove that they were independent and, in their eyes, strong.

God's idea of strong womanhood is a bit different from what the flappers promoted. He didn't design women to be in competition with men but rather to find their strength in something entirely different—their femininity.

Woman is inherently strong because God made her. Eve became weak when she listened to the serpent and doubted her Creator. And that's what weakens women today.

- We are told to exploit our sexuality.
- We are told to downplay our femininity.
- We are told to be anything *we* want.
- We are told that women are better than men.
- We are told that chivalry is offensive.
- We are told that girls rule.

Listening to the lies of the culture won't make us stronger, but weaker.

We dress ourselves with strength by embracing our God-given femininity. That is a place only we can fill. We don't need to try to imitate the place men have to fill. God created us differently and wonderfully. The strength of both male and female lies in their creative design. And only the God who made us has the right to tell us how that works.

Every day you and the women around you are being attacked by the same enemy who confronted Eve. God wants you to refuse the lies and be a reflection of the truth by embracing His image in a strong, feminine way. Mentor the young women around you. Celebrate the beauty and womanly ways you see in them. Gather with women in your church and school groups who can affirm you in your desire to bless the world through the distinct modality into which you were placed—a woman who knows her purpose and how to fill it.

Creator God, I accept the assignment of femininity You have given me. Teach me how to embrace it and reflect You well with it. Help me to honor the place of men and never believe I need to compete with them to be strong. In Jesus' name, amen.

Light

She perceives that her merchandise is profitable.
Her lamp does not go out at night.
PROVERBS 31:18 ESV

Women are often associated with light. Light is both illuminating and warming.

In the days when the American West was being settled, men often went ahead of women and children to choose sites for cabins or to lay railroad lines. They created rough, raw settlements in wilderness places. But when the women came, so did refinement. They illuminated the need for things that men would have done without. They brought the warmth of lamplight and fireside to lonely outposts.

The writer of this proverb about the virtuous woman said that her lamp doesn't go out at night. His meaning may be that she works late, but it could also be that she makes sure everything in her home is well supplied.

Remember the parable Jesus told about the wise and foolish maidens? Those who were wise had brought extra oil so they could refill their lamps as they waited for the wedding ceremony to begin. God always commends us for being prepared, in both earthly and heavenly ways.

As women, we need to be prepared for the darkness around us, culturally and spiritually. Satan will try to distract us so that we will ignore the light of the Holy Spirit within us. Thus we must stay on our guard.

In his letter to the Philippian church, Paul wrote that we should be "blameless and innocent, children of God without blemish in the midst of a crooked and twisted generation, among whom you shine as lights in the world" (Philippians 2:15 ESV).

Men are light-bearers too. All of us have the responsibility to shine the light of truth and grace onto those around us. In doing so, we reflect our Lord, who said, "I am the light of the world. Whoever follows me will not walk in darkness, but will have the light of life" (John 8:12 ESV).

Dear Jesus, I want to reflect You to those around me. As I live my life today as a Christian woman, show me the ways I can shine so that others may come to You. Amen.

Domesticity

She puts her hands to the distaff,
and her hands hold the spindle.
PROVERBS 31:19 ESV

Cooking shows today have taken over popular culture. Everyone considers himself or herself a chef just looking for a kitchen. Live, timed cooking contests are popular fare. The newest cookbooks from our favorite celebrities sell multiple copies. Domesticity is for everyone.

While there is certainly nothing wrong with men in the kitchen (and my husband has done a lot of cooking throughout our marriage), there is still something to be said about a mom-cooked meal. One of the things that makes me happiest is hearing my college-age children rejoice about being home to eat my food.

Proverbs 31:19 isn't speaking of food but of the preparation of cloth. In ancient times, it was a tedious process from start to finish, from the sheep's wool to the garment. It required time and commitment. It was a woman's job.

A lot has been said about why we shouldn't have "men's work" and "women's work," and I understand the concern about stereotypes that have no good basis. But I also believe we must recognize that some tasks appeal more to one gender than the other.

Today this verse might be interpreted as "She takes the children on a school clothes shopping trip." Although I see dads in stores with kids, most of the time it's the mom who is taking items off the racks and helping children try them on. Does this mean that a dad can't do it? No, only that it may more naturally appeal to a woman.

What the writer intended for us to pick up in this chapter written so long ago is that the woman who is to be commended makes sure the domestic tasks around the house are done. She doesn't wait for someone else to do them. She is on the job, ready to check items off her list.

If your husband helps with cooking and shopping, that's great. With the intensity of our lives today, we have to help carry the responsibilities of the home. But let's not forget to make sure the homes we have are properly cared for.

Dear Father, help me to be a good home manager of all the tasks that need to be done. Guide me so that I can accomplish the list I have today. Amen.

Compassion

*She opens her hand to the poor and
reaches out her hands to the needy.*
PROVERBS 31:20 ESV

- Florence Nightingale was called the "lady with the lamp" because of her care of soldiers.
- Catherine Booth was an integral part of founding the Salvation Army with her husband.
- Corrie ten Boom was the leader of a resistance group who rescued Jews in Holland.

Women have long been leaders in compassionate ministry to others. Perhaps the female hormone that makes us nurture babies and children also softens our hearts toward those in need. Men are often involved in caring for others too, and they have certain gifts in these areas that we do not. But there is no substitute for women reaching out their hands to the needy.

Jesus told us that helping others is the same as helping Him.

"For I was hungry and you gave me food, I was thirsty and you gave me drink, I was a stranger and you welcomed me, I was naked and you clothed me, I was sick and you visited me, I was in prison and you came to me." Then the righteous will answer him, saying, "Lord, when did we see you hungry and feed you, or thirsty and give you drink? And when did we see you a stranger and welcome you, or naked and clothe you? And when did we see you sick or in prison and visit you?" And the King will answer them, "Truly, I say to you, as you did it to one of the least of these my brothers, you did it to me." Matthew 25:35–40 ESV

The woman in the Proverbs 31 tribute didn't spend her days feathering her own nest, so to speak. She had eyes to see and a heart that cared, and she did what she could.

There are things and people in our world for which we need open eyes: sex trafficking, abortive and postabortive women, battered women, substance abuse addicts, single moms.

All of these women need the love of Jesus and the heart of a friend. Some of us don't have opportunities to be involved in actual outreach. But we can pray and give and care. Part of the unexpected loveliness of a woman of God is her compassion for others. Let's model it today.

Heavenly Father, there are so many hurting women in Your world. Show me how to be a conduit of love and grace in some way today. Amen.

Organization

She is not afraid of snow for her household,
for all her household are clothed in scarlet.
PROVERBS 31:21 ESV

Marie Kondo took the world by storm with her new philosophy and techniques for home organization. I know a lot of women were helped with her no-nonsense approach. Most of us have too much stuff anyway but just need a little help deciding what to keep and what not to keep.

In biblical times, most women didn't have that kind of problem. They didn't have the amount of belongings we have today, so storage wasn't an issue. But we do read in Proverbs 31:21 that the woman of the house did have her clothing organized. In fact, she ensured that all in her household were clothed appropriately. Some commentators believe that the word *scarlet* here refers to a specific type of warm clothing that she provided to everyone in her home—family and staff.

Organizing and making sure everyone has what he or she needs is a full-time job. We begin to get a sense for how busy this woman was! Yet most of the women I know are busy like that. My women friends juggle a lot of activities and responsibilities and accomplish a whole lot!

In a spiritual sense, we as mothers should be aware of the "clothing" our children are wearing. We want them to be clothed with Christ, to be wearing the righteousness He gives. As we provide for their earthly needs, let's not forget to monitor their heavenly needs as well. How tragic it would be if they were bountifully prepared for every kind of physical situation but naked and destitute spiritually!

Heavenly Father, Your grace in me will enable me to organize my life and prioritize the things that are most important. Help me always to be aware of my children's spiritual condition and never to forget to pray for them. In the name of Jesus, amen.

Beauty

She makes bed coverings for herself;
her clothing is fine linen and purple.
PROVERBS 31:22 ESV

It is sometimes thought that women who follow Christ should not care about beauty. But that is wrong. Our womanly beauty is a gift we are to steward well, and the writer of Proverbs 31 had something to say about it.

Appropriate self-care is part of the godly woman's routine. She knows that a sloppy, unkempt woman brings glory to no one, especially not to Christ. She is able to make good fashion choices and appropriate beauty statements because she understands how they fit in with the rest of her life as a follower of Christ.

Men were designed to image strength; women were created to reflect our Creator's beauty. God poured Himself into two human image bearers who, together, would make up an earthly depiction of His attributes. He made them as a pair, as complements. Two men do not make the right image. Neither do two women. Together a man and a woman make the perfect image of Christ and His bride, the church.

On a previous day, we learned about Lydia, the woman who sold purple goods. She was probably a well-to-do businesswoman, for that kind of merchandise was expensive and sought after. Purple was a fabric of the well dressed.

The words *fine linen* here suggest that this woman had good taste in her choices of fabric for clothing. She had elegant opinions and dressed herself accordingly.

Wherever beauty abounds, Satan will try to destroy it. He hates it because it reminds him of the One who made it. Satan tries to get women today to believe lies about their appearance. Either he suggests they make it their main focus, or he convinces them they aren't worth anything anyway and shouldn't even try. Both lies are destructive. The right attitude toward beauty is a surrender of it to the One who made it and a focus on using it to reflect glory back to Him. This is the attitude of the godly woman, the one who can wear fine linen and purple in the right way.

Lord, I want my womanly beauty to be an offering back to You.
I want it to honor Your image. Today, help me choose my
attitude and my clothing in such a way that everyone
who sees me knows I belong to You. Amen.

Respect

*Her husband is known in the gates when
he sits among the elders of the land.*

PROVERBS 31:23 ESV

Remember the story of Ruth? What a great romance!

After her first husband died, Ruth left her native country with her mother-in-law. They traveled back to Bethlehem in Judah, Naomi's hometown. When they arrived, Ruth went to work in the wheat fields, gleaning behind the harvesters so she and Naomi would have food to eat. And she "happened" to work in the fields of Boaz, a wealthy bachelor landowner. He noticed her, all right. And you'll remember that, under Naomi's instruction, she went to the threshing floor and asked him to "redeem" her or, we would say, marry her. It was a totally different culture then, and this was an appropriate request from a woman in her situation. Remember what happened next in the story? Boaz went to the city gate where the men transacted business to meet with the other guy who could also marry Ruth if he wanted.

This verse in Proverbs refers to that custom. The city gate was the town hall of the day. The men gathered there for official business. And if a man was recognized in the city gate, it was because he was greatly respected and prominent.

We're not told exactly why this husband was known at the city gate, but since the chapter deals with his wife, it is possible that her reputation as an excellent woman contributed to his respect in the city. She brought him honor too. This meshes perfectly with the words of Proverbs 12:4 (ESV): "An excellent wife is the crown of her husband, but she who brings shame is like rottenness in his bones."

If you're a married woman, think today about how you can be a crown to the man God gave you. It's just another way to glorify the Creator.

Father God, I want to bring honor to You and to the husband You've given me. Help me to be the excellent woman Your Word commends. In Jesus' name, amen.

Giftedness

She makes linen garments and sells them;
she delivers sashes to the merchant.
PROVERBS 31:24 ESV

I am a terrible seamstress. Sewing is definitely not one of my gifts! Or maybe the trouble is that I never intentionally developed it. My mother is very skilled with a sewing machine, but I did not seem to inherit that proclivity. I took home economics in high school, but my projects were not noteworthy. I made a few Easter dresses for my two little girls, but reading the patterns and putting together collar facings about did me in! I decided to focus on other areas of ability!

I'm glad the writer of Proverbs 31 wasn't saying that a woman has to know how to sew to be an excellent woman! A lot of us wouldn't make it.

Do you know where your gifts lie? I don't mean your spiritual gifts, although those are important. I mean your artistic gifts, the creative side of you.

I firmly believe that God puts artistry into all of us somehow. It's another way we bear His image. He is a God of creativity; He puts a little bit of it into each of us. And I believe that we will use those creative gifts in eternity too. After all, we only use our bodies to express what's inside. When we have new glorified bodies, imagine what we'll be able to do!

Set out to discover what you're good at if you don't already know. Ask friends. Ask your mom. Be aware of what area of the store you wander to first. What kinds of boards do you like on Pinterest? What pastimes interest you? Decorating? Baking? Flower arranging? Painting? Sculpting? Writing? Composing? Something else?

Find out what lights you up inside and try to work it into your schedule. You will be a richer person if you are creating. And like this woman, you might even turn your craft into a home business.

Father, thank You for putting Your creativity inside me.
Today I ask that You would help me use my gifts for
Your glory and for my good. Amen.

Security

Strength and dignity are her clothing,
and she laughs at the time to come.
PROVERBS 31:25 ESV

Every woman I know wants to be confident. We want that inner assurance that we are enough, that we are capable and beautiful, that we have something to offer.

We've talked about strength and how we gain it by embracing the woman God made each of us to be. And when we do that, we also discover the dignity of living in proper balance with the rest of God's world.

Insecurities hound every woman. No matter how accomplished she looks or how successful she is, inside she wonders. We all do. That's why the lie the serpent told Eve is so diabolical. He said that she would be like a god (Genesis 3:5). But what really happened is that she lost her security as well as her innocence. She knew the difference between good and evil after that, and she began to be plagued by fears and doubts and all the other negative emotions that are part of our world because of sin.

The way back to security is found in embracing the truth instead of lies. And we do this by getting close to our Creator and reading His Word.

A woman who knows she was made by the hand of God and created for a special purpose can hold her head up even when things go wrong and even when she doesn't like something about herself. She realizes that God is working out a plan through her and that even her deficiencies somehow are part of that.

Such a woman can laugh at the future, not in a mocking, foolish, irresponsible way but in a trusting, joyful way. She knows that God holds everything in His hands and that He has the final say. She doesn't have to try to figure everything out when she trusts the One who knows all. "He has made everything beautiful in its time. Also, he has put eternity into man's heart, yet so that he cannot find out what God has done from the beginning to the end" (Ecclesiastes 3:11 ESV).

Father in heaven, You hold all things in Your hands, and You made everything, including me. Today I trust You for my future, and I find my strength and dignity in following Your purpose. Amen.

Kindness

She opens her mouth with wisdom,
and the teaching of kindness is on her tongue.
PROVERBS 31:26 ESV

Professor Higgins in *My Fair Lady* declares that he can recognize a lady by her speech. He then sets out to prove that he can, conversely, make a lady out of a "guttersnipe" by teaching her proper English. The process is amusing and somewhat traumatizing for poor Eliza Doolittle.

Whether Higgins could actually peg a lady by her speech, we're not sure. But we do know that one can tell a godly woman by the kindness of her words.

We live in a very uncivil time. Everyday speech has become crude and crass; words for bodily functions that would never have been condoned in previous generations are now used with barely a blink of the eye. Conversations about intimacy and sexuality are common. Political discussions dissolve into verbal brawls on social media. We are becoming a generation without decorum and kindness.

In such a setting, a godly woman is refreshingly different. She guards her words and uses wisdom in the topics on which she converses. And above all, she is kind in her speech.

Kindness is more than not saying something rude or offensive; it is framing words in such a way that a message doesn't come across as hurtful or demeaning.

The excellent woman knows that the words she says reflect on the Lord she represents. His honor is worth more than her having a cheap parting shot. His agenda is more important than hers. His truth and love must be the standards for her conversations.

In the end, Professor Higgins did successfully transform Eliza into a lady. But it was her falling in love with him that made the most difference; she wanted to be transformed so she could please him and be in his world. And so it is with us. When we love the Lord, we are happy to be transformed into what pleases Him.

Father, I want to be a woman who uses wisdom and kindness in my conversations. I want to make Your heart glad with the way I speak. I ask You to help with that today. In Jesus' name, amen.

Nurturing

She looks well to the ways of her household
and does not eat the bread of idleness.
Proverbs 31:27 esv

If you've ever seen a mother bird preparing her nest, you have an idea of what nurturing is all about. She flies back and forth, gathering twigs and leaves and bits of fur and brush, trip after trip, adding to the little home where her young will be hatched.

I remember going through the "nesting" days before my first child was born. I had an unexplainable urge to get everything ready. For me, that meant I was out in the grocery store on the day before her birth, waddling down the aisles, putting quick-fix food in my cart. Some women paint rooms or do deep cleaning; others cook and freeze meals. It's part of the instinctual, hormonal response to the motherhood that's about to begin.

Nurturing is both a natural and a learned skill. Most women with normal hormones have maternal feelings and responses. At times these can be damaged through trauma or impaired through chemical imbalance. But the norm is for women to be inclined to nurture. Such is the effect of estrogen and progesterone in our bodies.

The excellent woman of Proverbs leaned into the way God made her and nurtured the people around her. For us, nurturing may be with chocolate chip cookies, or it may be with a counseling session in a daughter's room. There are many ways to nurture, and the wise woman uses them all.

Some of my precious memories of time spent with my own mother took place in my bedroom after I'd finished my homework and she came in to sit and talk and laugh with me. We'd talk over all kinds of things, and that time together created a deep bond that I cherish today. She nurtured me as a daughter, as a woman, as a person. The insight and intuition God gave her allowed her to see the things I needed her to see and say the things I needed her to say. That is the beauty of this calling to nurture.

Today, look around your home and let your mom gut speak to you. You may see someone who needs nurturing before the day is done.

Dear God, You do all things well, and You created me with this ability to nurture others. Show me how I can use it for the good of those around me. Amen.

Mother

Her children rise up and call her blessed;
her husband also, and he praises her.
PROVERBS 31:28 ESV

Proverbs 31:28 is the poster verse for Mother's Day services everywhere. It's a good one.

I've always been intrigued by the wording. It sounds so ceremonial. Today we don't usually say that we will "rise up" to do anything. But it also sounds so special and rewarding! This woman's children and husband praise her publicly and commend her wonderful worth.

The quintessential mother figure for years was Caroline Ingalls of *Little House on the Prairie* fame, or at least the screen version of her played by Karen Grassle. She was soft spoken, kind, nurturing, domestic, wise, strong, resourceful, and gentle. She knew when to sit down on the side of the bed for a talk with Laura. She knew when to raise her eyebrows at Charles to signal to him that they needed to have a conversation about the children. She knew when to invite the neighbors over and how to make a delicious meal out of almost nothing. She kept the family grounded while Charles fought the battles of the prairie and the Indians and the various other crises that arose.

While we may smile a bit at the idea that we think of an actress as a model of motherhood, it is nonetheless true that authors and screenwriters may infuse a script with traits that they remember from their own mothers or traits that they themselves value in womanhood. Certainly Laura Ingalls Wilder, the author of the original *Little House* books, held her own mother in high regard. This often came through in the way she described her in the home and in her interaction with the family.

You may not fit the mold of Caroline Ingalls, but you can embody the traits of a godly woman and be the mother your family needs. The verse doesn't say what they are praising, only that they are. Within the creative range of our God, there are mothers with all variety of gifts and abilities, attributes and preferences, styles, attitudes, and manners. But all of us can love our children and live out, to our best understanding and ability, a life of sacrifice and service that, someday, they will appreciate.

Heavenly Father, thank You for the gift of mothers. Thank You for my mother and for the children You've given me. I want to live in such a way that my life will make a positive difference in theirs. Amen.

Relationship

*"Many women have done excellently, but you
surpass them all." Charm is deceitful, and beauty is vain,
but a woman who fears the LORD is to be praised.*
PROVERBS 31:29–30 ESV

Overall, the most important thing about the excellent woman is her relationship with God.

The entirety of Proverbs 31 on the excellent woman points to verse 30. All of these attributes that set her apart and make her a wonderful person are there because she is in touch with her Creator and has a relationship with Him.

What does it mean to fear the Lord?

- The fear of the Lord is the beginning of wisdom (Psalm 111:10).
- The fear of the Lord is the beginning of knowledge (Proverbs 1:7).
- The fear of the Lord is to hate evil (Proverbs 8:13).
- The fear of the Lord prolongs life (Proverbs 10:27).
- The fear of the Lord gives strong confidence (Proverbs 14:26).
- The fear of the Lord is a fountain of life (Proverbs 14:27).

To fear the Lord is to acknowledge His sovereignty and live with reverence for His authority over us. A woman who does this understands much about her purpose in this world. She is listening for the voice of her God and trying to reflect Him in everything she does. That is why she does things excellently. That is why her relationship with Him is more vital than earthly beauty or charm. The outer beauty perishes, but the inner beauty is unfading (see 1 Peter 3:4).

Heavenly Father, my understanding of You and my relationship with You shape the woman I am. Give me grace this day to live in Your light and love. Amen.

Reward

Give her of the fruit of her hands,
and let her works praise her in the gates.
PROVERBS 31:31 ESV

Better than fireworks or applause or trophies, the words "Well done" are an eternal reward.

The gates of a city were where important announcements were made. Business transactions were conducted there in ancient times. They were the town hall, the hub of events and activities. When the writer of Proverbs 31 said that the excellent woman would be praised in the gates, it was an acknowledgment that the whole city would hear the praise this woman received. And how would that happen? People would be talking about her because of the "fruit of her hands." In the Bible, "fruit" often refers to the works we do. So this woman would be known for her excellent character and remarkable works, and even those conducting business at the city gates would mention her name. That was pretty amazing in a day when women weren't especially valued or discussed. It was a great reward.

But even better than that is a reward to which every godly woman can look forward. A great day is coming when we will all stand before the throne of God. Our works will be examined, and rewards will be given. "For we must all appear before the judgment seat of Christ, so that each one may receive what is due for what he has done in the body, whether good or evil" (2 Corinthians 5:10 ESV).

The godly woman will have no greater joy than to hear words of commendation from her Lord. Maybe they will be something like these words from Jesus' parable: "Well done, good and faithful servant. You have been faithful over a little; I will set you over much. Enter into the joy of your master" (Matthew 25:21 ESV).

Dear heavenly Father, someday I will stand before You, and I want You to be pleased with how I reflected You on earth. Help me to live my life with eternity in view. In Jesus' name, amen.

More Much-Needed Encouragement for Your Growing Faith

Unafraid / 978-1-64352-415-3
Untroubled / 978-1-68322-946-9
Unashamed / 978-1-64352-192-3
Unhurried / 978-1-68322-599-7
Unfinished / 978-1-68322-747-2

These delightful devotionals will refresh and renew your spirit, filling your heart with the assurance that only God can provide today and for all your days to come!

Hardcover / $12.99 each